Preface

The practice of Hinduism varies in different regions of India and in different sections of society in the same region. Village Hinduism is different from the middle-class urban variety and the practice of the faith outside India is modified and adapted to suit social and economic conditions overseas. This variety in practice makes it impossible to include the whole spectrum of Hinduism in one book. Indeed, it is said that there are as many Hinduisms as there are Hindus.

Yet the practical side of the faith reflects its theological, philosophical and social aspects, and for that reason I have chosen an imaginary Brahmin family of priestly background, whose members are more likely to observe elaborate rituals, in order to show as fully as possible how Hinduism is practised. Hinduism is absorbed through observation and participation, and the grandparental role in a family is important; elders pass on traditions by involving members of their family in the prescribed rituals of religious festivals and sacraments, thus ensuring continuity. Interdependence and authority are the two principles which underlie family relationships and activities; major decisions are taken by the whole group while each member has a specific area of authority and responsibility. It is hoped that the dramatic sections of this book will help to highlight the way family members develop an awareness of their duties and accept the need for carrying them out.

I have tried to cover a large area of Hindu practice, by including descriptions of the actual performance of various rituals, conversations between members of the family, letters to show regional and overseas variation, and accounts of lectures by learned scholars, while taking into consideration certain innovations suggested by the younger generation.

Sanskrit and other Indian words are italicised and diacritics are used to help pronunciation. (The vowel 'a' should be sounded like 'u' in 'urgent' and 'ā' like 'a' in 'car'; 'ū' is like 'u' in rude; 'u' is like 'u' in 'put'; 'ī' is like 'i' in 'machine'; 'e' is like 'ai' in 'wait' and 'o' is like 'o' in 'hope'. The other vowel sounds approximate English usage.)

My sincere thanks are due to the editorial staff of The Saint Andrew Press for their caring criticism of the script; to Mrs Barbara Nelson-Smith for the meticulous care taken by her in the preparation of the typescript; and to my wife, Dr Helen Kanitkar, for her erudite comments and constant encouragement.

I hope the reader will find my small effort helpful in understanding the Hindu tradition.

V P (Hemant) Kanitkar
New Barnet, Hertfordshire, 1987

Introduction

I am Ābā. Of course, that is my nickname, a short form of *Ajobā*, meaning grandfather. I was named Nārāyan, and when I married, my wife was given a new name by her new family. She was called Laxmi. Very few people refer to us as Nārāyan and Laxmi nowadays. We are simply Ābā and Ājī, grandpa and grandma. We live in a small town called Wāi, so for generations our family name has been Wāiker. This is quite common with many families in Western India. The suffix '*-ker*' is added to the name of the place where they live; so there are family names such as Puneker, Bhorker, Parker and Kanitkar. We are Hindus living a way of life that has evolved through many modifications and changes over a period of 4000 years. We have much in our society that needs changing and those changes are taking place—a little faster, perhaps, since our nation achieved independence in 1947. But I also believe there is much in our way of life that would be helpful to other people with different cultural traditions in other parts of the world.

I am now 65 and have been a pensioner for the past ten years. I passed the Matriculation Examination in 1937 and became a clerk in the civil court two years later. My father, being a priest, did not have much money to send me to college, but he owned our house, which I inherited when he died. I worked hard at my job and eventually I retired as a head clerk. My salary was sufficient to clothe and feed a family of six and to educate my four children, two boys and two girls. My wife, Laxmi, has had to work hard bringing up our children and looking after the home. She is in good health at 61, but now she is able to relax a little, since our two daughters-in-law share the responsibility of housework. This is just as well, since there are 11 people living in the house.

My eldest son Govind is 42, and his wife Yamū is 41. Govind is a strongly built man of five foot seven, which is above average for a Brahmin in Mahārāshtra in Western India. I was able to send him to Poatdar College in Bombay where he obtained a degree in commerce and worked in a bank in Bombay for about eight years. He had to live in two small rooms in a tenement *chawl* (block of flats) in the suburbs at Kurla. He was not very happy there, so I suggested that he should re-train and become a priest at Wāi. I am glad he took my advice and spent five years at a private Sanskrit school, because now he practises as a priest, earning a good living; and, more importantly, he is happy in his work. I am pleased to see that he is able to preserve our cultural and religious tradition which is threatened by the lack of Sanskrit teaching in our schools. Three years ago he took in two pupils who are learning the different forms of Hindu worship and they will be able to carry on the tradition after Govind.

I often feel that there should be a standard course of studies and a final examination for all Hindu priests. The absence of such a course produces priests with varying scholarships, some of whom follow the *Vedic* and others the *Puranic* tradition. Be that as it may, I have spent many an afternoon listening to Govind and his two pupils as they chant the various Sanskrit *mantras*, and I have enjoyed the musical richness of the language.

Govind's wife, Yamū, is also a graduate and gives private tuition to half a dozen girls from the high school. Yamū has a fair complexion with black hair and light brown eyes. She is a modest daughter-in-law and a devoted wife and mother. Their elder son, Vasant, now 18, is studying at his father's old college and wants to work in a bank when he qualifies. Gitā, their daughter, is beautiful like her mother and is studying in the Girls' High School. She is to appear for the Secondary School Certificate (SSC) examination next year. I did say that there are 11 people living in the house, but that is not strictly true, because Vasant is away at college in Bombay. However, he comes home during his vacations.

Now to my second son and his family. Gopāl is healthy enough but slightly built and of average height. He is darker skinned, with black hair and pale grey eyes. He went to college at Puné and read English and Marāthi, our mother tongue. After taking a teaching degree, he came back to Wāi and now teaches at the Boys' High School. His wife, Rādhā, whom he met while at college and who is also a graduate, has a part-time job at the Girls' High School. She comes from a good family and, although she was the daughter of a rich cloth merchant in Puné, she has adapted well to our modest household. Rādhā, like Yamū, my other daughter-in-law, is respectful to her elders and a devoted wife and mother, but she is a little less patient with her children, particularly the two daughters Tārā and Leenā.

Gopāl's eldest son, Ramesh, is very big for his age and at 15 is showing great promise in his studies as well as sports. He is a good swimmer and likes cricket. He may well play for Mahārāshtra in the Ranji Trophy competition. That is a loving grandfather's future dream. But now Ramesh is at the Boys' High School and will appear for the SSC examination next year. Gopāl's elder daughter Tārā is 11, and the younger, Leenā, is just eight. Both have bright shining eyes, are quick to learn and are full of questions that demand logical answers. This makes me very optimistic about the future of our way of life. The younger generation of new India is not prepared to accept the Hindu tradition without questioning outmoded practices, and this attitude will bring about the necessary changes for improvement without uprooting the whole system. Laxmi and I are often filled with joy when we spend at least an hour every evening with Tārā and Leenā, telling them some story or other, or teaching them simple Marāthi verses, or indeed, listening to them as they read from their school text books.

My elder daughter, Neelā, now in her early 30s, is married to Ganesh, and has only one child, a daughter named Sheila. They live in a large city in England called Leicester. Ganesh went to Sir JJ School of Art in Bombay where he studied architecture. After qualifying, he could not get a job where he could satisfy his creative talents, so, borrowing money from his uncle, he went to the United Kingdom, and through the help of his friends in England he managed to get a job in Leicester. Neelā and Ganesh visit us every four years. Sheila, my English granddaughter, was born in Leicester, and when she came here last time I think she found our small town very hot and dusty and our lifestyle rather primitive.

Sometimes I compare Govind's life with that of Ganesh. Govind had a good job in a bank but because of poor living conditions in Kurla he came back to our roomy house and became a priest to find happiness in his work. Ganesh, on the other hand, qualified in Bombay but had to go outside India to find a rewarding job. Nonetheless, Ganesh, Neelā and Sheila are Hindus, no matter in what style they live or where. But it is a pity that India has lost so many of her brightest children to England because of lack of opportunity here.

My younger daughter, Latā, also went to college in Pune. After getting a BA degree, she studied for a diploma to become a librarian and she met her husband, Mādhav, while still at college. She told me about him, his family and their caste. I asked our friends in Puné to make suitable enquiries and eventually their marriage took place. It was not really an arranged marriage for they had already chosen each other. However, we were very happy to complete the formalities and I knew Mādhav's parents approved of Latā.

Latā is 30 and Mādhav four years older. They have well paid jobs in the Central Library at Delhi. They have an eight year old son, Mohan, who speaks in Marāthi with his parents, in Hindi with his neighbourhood friends, and goes to an English-Medium Convent School in Delhi.

Now that I have told you briefly about myself, my children and grandchildren, I am going to describe our home in Wāi.

You have to climb two stone steps from the street and, on entering the front door, climb down two more steps into our front courtyard, which is about 18 foot square. There is a six foot wide covered verandah to your right, and at the street-end, there is the lavatory with a septic tank which is periodically emptied by the town's municipality. Facing you is our main sitting room. One side of this room, as well as one side of the verandah, is completely open, with supporting wooden pillars on stone bases. This provides us with ventilation but protects us during the Monsoons. There are three similar rooms behind the sitting room, each 22 foot long and ten foot wide, all connected with teak doors. The last of these opens out into the back courtyard where there is a well. The second and third rooms are multi-purpose, since they are used as sitting rooms or store rooms during the day, and as bedrooms at night. The fourth room is the kitchen and dining room. There is a smaller room, about eight foot square, built as an extension and opening out onto the back courtyard, which is used for taking our daily baths. The stone floor is ideal for this bathing room, because we can splash water without feeling guilty or causing any damage. The floor dries within an hour. The floors in other rooms are of mud-plaster, which is also used for the walls. We have two rooms on the first floor, which are used by my sons and their wives. Ramesh sleeps in the first room on the ground floor, the three girls use the second room, and Laxmi and I use the third. When Vasant comes home he sleeps in the sitting room. Every evening after our meal we have to set up mosquito-nets over thin mattresses spread on the floor.

The walls of our house are of mud-brick and the roof is of kiln-baked red tiles. The ceilings are made of sturdy wooden joists, beams and planks, and the floors in the upstairs rooms are of mud-plaster. The materials used for our house do not absorb heat; they keep the house very cool and ventilated in temperatures of over 110 degrees Fahrenheit. Forty years ago we had no electricity or radio; our water had to be drawn from the well in the back courtyard, and we burned wood in the mud-stove for cooking. Things have certainly improved in recent years. We use cylinder-gas and metal rings for cooking. There is piped water, radio and electric light. All windows have iron bars and wooden shutters but no glass panes. There is no mains drainage as yet, but the irrigation dam five miles west of Wāi, on the river Krishnā, provides us with ample water all the year round.

Although my English suffices, it is not very good, so I have requested my friend Mr Hemant Kanitkar to describe in detail how we spend our year. I am sure you will agree with me, after you have read this book, that our way of life has much to offer the rich countries of Europe and America to enable them to understand that *Dharma* (one's moral duty) is the way to personal liberation, and that *Ahimsā*—non-injury and tolerance—is the key to world peace.

1

New Year, Rāma-Navami, Rāmāyana

Ābā woke up at five o'clock as usual. 'Are you awake?' he asked Ājī. 'Yes,' she replied. Both sat up on their bed on the floor and said a prayer asking forgiveness of Mother Earth for placing upon her their physical burden. 'O Prithivi, consort of Vishnu, you who wear a sari in the form of Seven Seas and have mountains for ornaments, please forgive us for touching you with our feet.' Each bowed reverently, putting their joined palms close to their bodies and touching their foreheads with the tips of the first finger. Ābā went to brush his teeth while Ājī folded the bed sheets and counterpanes and rolled up the mattresses. Within half an hour both were seated on wooden boards on the floor in the kitchen sipping hot tea which Ājī had spiced with crushed, fresh ginger.

This was a special day for the Wāiker family, as it was to all Hindus, for it was the first day of the first month of the Hindu calendar. All Hindus in this sleepy, dusty town in Western India would welcome the New Year in the traditional manner. Whatever the city folk did to start the New Year by way of celebrations, people in small towns and villages still observed the traditional rituals. The Hindu New Year usually falls in March, when there is a distinct chill in the air, and this is a reason for the rich food that is prepared for the mid-day meal.

'This ginger tea is tasty and you make it so well,' Ābā complimented his wife.

'I like to prepare our morning tea the way you like it. That is the only thing I prepare these days because Yamū and Rādhā do most of the cooking,' Ājī said.

'They will need your help for today's meal.'

'Yes, but I shall only be allowed to prepare the sweet dish for today's feast. I tell you, they have between them taken over my kitchen completely,' Ājī added, with a certain amount of pride, satisfaction and relief.

Their conversation was disturbed as Yamū, Rādhā and their husbands got up and came into the kitchen. The brothers, Govind and Gopāl, sat down while Yamū and Rādhā began preparing tea and setting out cups and saucers. Ājī went into the middle room to see if Tārā and Leenā were awake. Both the girls were fast asleep, but Gitā, Govind's daughter, stirred and opened her eyes.

'Gitā,' said Ājī, 'you and these two will have to get up soon. Have your tea and quickly take a bath after the men.'

'But Ājī,' said Gitā, sleepily, 'we don't have school today. We have a holiday because it is New Year's day.'

'That is why you must hurry, my dear, otherwise you will not be able to take part when we raise the banner and perform *pūjā*,' Ājī said as she went into the front room to awaken Ramesh. But Ramesh was already up, and helping his father, Gopāl, to unfasten the long bamboo pole that hung horizontally under the eaves. Ājī watched them for a few minutes and went back into the middle room. The girls were now up and busy folding the sheets and bed covers and rolling up the mattresses.

In the kitchen there was a little conference which Ājī joined and soon the six grown-ups were discussing the menu for the mid-day feast. For the next hour or so the Walker household was a hive of activity; its members were busy either having tea or attending to their morning preparations.

Ājī supervised the children, making sure that they wore their new clothes after bathing. By this time Gopāl had washed the bamboo pole and Ramesh and Gitā were tying a small brass pot, a colourful new piece of cloth about four feet long, a garland of fresh flowers and a string of sugar discs to one end of the pole. Ābā and Ājī were the last to take their baths and, when they had finished, Govind wore his silk *dhoti* (loin-cloth) and Yamū prepared a large brass plate with the pūjā articles on it, which included red and yellow powders, rice grains, fresh flowers, some betel leaves and small coins, a betel nut, two joss-sticks, a small ghee lamp with an upright wick and a box of matches.

'Where is the sandalwood paste and the second garland of flowers?' asked Ābā.

'Ramesh and Gitā are getting those things ready,' Rādhā told him, while adjusting the belt on Leenā's new frock. Ājī, Yamū and Rādhā all wore new saris.

When Ramesh and Gitā had prepared the missing articles, everyone gathered in the front room. Govind applied the sandal-wood paste, red and yellow powders and some rice grains to the bottom end of the bamboo pole and tied the second garland of fresh flowers about five feet from the end. Then Govind and Gopāl raised the pole into an upright position and held it above the clean patch of ground in the front courtyard which Rādhā had earlier prepared. Ramesh then tied the pole to one of the pillars. The brass pot and the flower garland shone in the soft rays of the rising sun and the length of colourful cloth gently fluttered in the breeze. Govind lit the joss-sticks and the lamp and, uttering some *mantras*—sacred formulae—offered the light and the incense to the banner, and prayer for a successful and trouble-free year for the family. Each member of Āba's family offered flowers and *kum-kum* (red powder) to the banner. Ājī then distributed some milksweets to sweeten the beginning of the New Year.

The children showed off their new clothes when they went with Gopāl to the market to buy fresh vegetables. Āba and Govind tied a string of mango leaves across the top of their front door to welcome the New Year. The earlier menu-conference had decided to prepare *bāsundi*—a special sweet made from thickened milk, sugar, almonds and cardomom—and *puris* as the main feast dish, in addition to plain rice, vegetable curry, dāl and chilli-coriander chutney. The meal was prepared by Yamū and Rādhā but Ājī was asked to prepare *bāsundi*. There was a little bother with the gas cylinder, and the two daughters-in-law did not think it would last. However, Ājī decided to use the primus stove to prepare the special sweet and the meal was finally cooked. The cylinder ran out later in the afternoon, and the shop which supplied gas cylinders was shut, the New Year's day being a public holiday.

'These new inventions are so unreliable!' complained Ājī. 'We were much better off with a wood fire.'

'That is not really true, Ājī,' said Gitā, 'we don't have that thick smoke in the kitchen any more. A gas cylinder is better.'

'Don't worry, Mother,' assured Govind, 'we shall get the replacement cylinder tomorrow.'

Ābā had a short nap in the afternoon after a heavy lunch. But later, when he was having tea, Leenā was full of questions.

'Ābā, you know those people who live near the flour mill, Yusuf and Ismail Khan?'

'Yes,' said Ābā, 'what about them?'

'Well, they don't have a banner in their house like we have. Why is that?' Leenā wanted to know why the Khan family behaved differently.

'We have a banner because we are Hindus and we always welcome the New Year by having the pūjā in the morning.'

'But are they not Hindus?'

'No, Leenā, they are Muslims. They have a different way of celebrating the New Year.'

'Do you know what it is? Have you seen?'

'No. I have never been inside their house.' It was clear that Ābā was unable to satisfy Leenā's curiosity.

'Ābā,' continued Leenā, 'our teachers say that we are all Indians.'

'Yes, that is right,' replied Ābā, 'but we are also Hindus. We can be both, Indians and Hindus. People don't have to give up their beliefs to be Indians.'

The conversation came to an abrupt end when Rādhā called for the three girls. She wanted to take them with her to visit the Shiva temple near the river.

In about a week's time the festival of *Rāma-Navami* took place. Ābā and Ājī announced that they were going to observe a fast. Tārā was curious to learn why her grandparents were not going to eat anything that day.

'But Tārā, my dear,' said Ājī, 'we are going to eat *something*, but nothing made from rice, wheat or lentils. We shall have some fried sago with natural yogurt, a banana and a cup of milk.'

'Ājī, can I fast with you?' asked Leenā.

'Yes, but we shall not eat anything until after we return from the Rāma temple. Today is *Rāma-Navami* and there will be many people at the temple celebrating Rāma's birthday.'

'Can we come to the temple? We have half day school in the afternoon,' said Tārā and Leenā together. So Ābā and Ājī took their granddaughters to the Rāma temple.

As *Rāma-Navami* is a nativity festival, the resident priest at the temple had decorated a small brass swing-cot with fresh flowers, and he had placed a coconut in it which represented baby Rāma. At noon pūjā was offered to the marble image of Rāma, and *ārti* was performed, when devotional verses were sung as the priest offered light and incense to the deity. When the ārti dish, with a ghee lamp and ignited camphor, was taken round the congregation, people put small coins or one rupee notes in the dish, held their hands at a safe distance around the flames and touched their faces and hair to ward off evil from their lives. At the end of the pūjā, *prasād* (blessed offering) made from powdered ginger and castor sugar was distributed. Tārā and Leenā enjoyed the experience immensely and when they came home they had their fast-day food with Ābā and Ājī.

That day, Ābā, Ājī, Yamū, Rādhā and the two younger girls ate their special diet, but Govind, Gopāl, Ramesh and Gitā had their normal meal of rice and jowar bread with vegetable curry and dāl. Usually it is the women who observe fasting days in the Hindu tradition. Women do the housework, which requires a lot of effort and energy, and, furthermore, in villages, women do the heavy work in the fields. The special food allowed on various fasting days includes fresh fruit, ghee, milk and peanuts, all rich in proteins; thus observing fasting days is a subtle way of making sure that women have a periodic intake of nourishing food. Fasting days and feast days are widely observed in middle-class Hindu society, but farmers and artisans, too, observe the important festivals such as *Diwāli* and *Holi*.

Ābā had promised to tell the youngsters the story of Rāma, so when Tārā and Leenā returned from school, they had a snack of chapati and dry vegetable curry first and then they sat in the front room near Ābā and awaited his tale eagerly. Gitā also came to join them.

'In the country of the Kosalas at Ayodhyā, there ruled a powerful king called Dasharatha. The *Rāmāyana* is based on an ancient traditional story, at least 3000 years old, which is mostly legend but may have had some historical basis. The king had three wives, Kausalyā, the Senior Queen, Sumitrā and Kaikeyī. He was fond of hunting and, one night, while hunting in the woods, he shot his arrow in the direction of a faint sound which the king thought was made by a deer drinking water from a stream. As the king approached his kill, to his horror he found a dead boy with an arrow through his chest and a drinking vessel close by. Dasharatha filled the vessel with water and walked a few yards in the direction of human voices; there he found a blind couple calling their son's name, Shrāvan. "Have you brought water for us?" they asked.

' "Yes," the king replied softly, and, as he handed the pot to the man, his fingers touched the blind man's hand. The man shivered in fright.

' "Who are you? Where is our son, Shrāvan?"

'Dasharatha told them what had happened. The blind couple wailed with grief and just before they died from the shock they cursed Dasharatha: "You will die like us, grieving for your beloved son."

'The king attended to the funeral of the blind couple and their son, Shrāvan, and returned with his attendants to Ayodhyā, dejected and frightened.

'On another occasion Dasharatha was wounded in battle, but, nursed by his younger queen Kaikeyi, managed to achieve victory. He felt very pleased and granted Kaikeyi two boons. Kaikeyi thanked the king and said that she would demand the fulfilment of two wishes sometime in the future. As time went on, Dasharatha was very busy with the affairs of his kingdom, and as he became rich and more powerful, he forgot the incidents involving Shrāvan and Kaikeyi.

'The king was childless, so, on the advice of the royal priests, he performed a sacrifice and made offerings to Agni, the Fire-God. Agni, being pleased with the king's devotion, gave him a sacred potion and asked him to divide it equally between his three queens. The queens were given the sacred drink as instructed by Agni and in due course Kausalyā gave birth to Rāma, Sumitrā had twins—Lakshman and Shatrughna—while Bharat was born to Kaikeyi, the youngest queen. Dasharatha was overjoyed and his subjects celebrated the birth of the four princes.

'The four princes grew up to be handsome, strong and clever and progressed in their education under the guidance of the chief priest, Vasistha. They also learned the skill of archery, and Prince Rāma excelled his brothers in this branch of their education. They were sent to the hermitage of the sage Vishwāmitra to protect his sacrifices from the raids of demons, in which task Rāma and

Lakshman were successful and the sage was pleased with their performance. Here they were told that King Janaka of the Videha country was arranging an archery contest and the winner would marry the king's daughter, Sītā.'

'But Ābā,' interrupted Gītā, 'when our teacher told us this story, she used the word *Sītā-swyam-vara* and said that Sītā *chose* her future husband.'

'I think,' replied Ābā, 'the word *Swyam-vara* (self-choice) gives a wrong impression. Sītā was won by Rāma as a prize. She did not have the freedom to choose her husband.'

'Well, I shall certainly choose mine,' said Gītā.

'We shall see when you complete your education,' said Ābā. 'Now will you let me continue the story? In the archery contest, which King Janaka had arranged, all the assembled princes had to try to bend the God Shiva's bow and attach the string in position. Many princes tried in vain; even Rāvana, the powerful King of Lankā, failed miserably. Then it was Rāma's turn, and as Rāma picked up the bow in his powerful arms and bent it, it broke before he could attach the string in position. The whole assembly was amazed at Rāma's strength and congratulated the prince on his success with shouts of joy and spontaneous clapping.

'King Janaka was pleased and immediately announced that Sītā would be Rāma's wife. At once, the royal messengers from Videha were sent to Dasharatha, in Ayodhyā, giving him the news and inviting him to Mithilā for the wedding. Dasharatha, with royal priests and nobles and his queens, travelled to Mithilā where he was greeted by King Janaka.

'Janaka's capital, Mithilā, was decorated with garlands and banners, and when all the invited guests had assembled in the Palace, Vasishtha, the Chief Priest of Dasharatha, performed the wedding ceremony according to *Vedic* rites. In fact, as Rāma married Sītā, Lakshman was married to Sītā's sister, Urmilā; and Bharata and Shatrughna were married to Sītā's cousins, Māndavi and Shruta-Kirti respectively. After the wedding feast Dasharatha, with his queens, sons, and daughters-in-law, and all the members of his court, returned to Ayodhyā to a joyous welcome by the people.

'Rāma and his brothers were instructed by Vasishtha and other scholars in statecraft and princely duties and Rāma's virtues and royal graces delighted Dasharatha who decided to make Rāma his *yuva rāj*—heir-apparent. The decision was welcomed by the whole court and the people of Ayodhyā, but Queen Kaikeyi was against it. The queen's personal maid, called Manthara, had pointed out to Kaikeyi that if Rāma were to be crowned heir-apparent, her son, Bharata, would become a servant of the future king and she herself would have a subordinate position in the palace, even although King Dasharatha loved her more than Kausalyā or Sumitrā. Kaikeyi thought about Manthara's words, and remembering the king's former promise, decided to exact the fulfilment of two wishes. She refused to see Dasharatha, and when the king himself went to her chamber, Kaikeyi demanded the fulfilment of the two boons he granted long ago.

'The king had given his word and was duty bound to keep it. He spoke: "Name your two wishes, and they shall be fulfilled."

' "My first wish is for Bharata to be heir-apparent," said Kaikeyi.

' "And what is your second wish?" asked Dasharatha.

' "Banish Rāma from the kingdom for 14 years."

'Dasharatha was devastated but could do nothing. All preparations for Rāma's installation as heir-apparent were cancelled and Rāma was told by the king that he would be banished for 14 years. Rāma, in complete obedience to the king's commands, prepared to leave Ayodhyā; Sītā and Lakshman decided to go with him.

'Rāma left Ayodhyā, ignoring the people's pleas to stay, and he remained just outside the boundary of the kingdom for some time. On his departure, Dasharatha fell ill through grief for his eldest son and, as the illness took him to Death's door, he remembered the words of Shrāvan's blind parents: "You will die like us, grieving for your beloved son." When the king died, Prince Bharata went to meet Rāma and asked him to return to Ayodhyā, but Rāma refused. Bharata brought back Rāma's sandals and, keeping them on the throne, ruled as Regent, because he knew that Rāma, being the eldest son, was the rightful king.

'Rāma and his companions travelled south to Chitrakūta and then to the Dandaka forest where they lived for many years. There Sītā saw a spotted golden deer and asked Rāma to obtain it for her. Rāma went after the deer, asking Lakshman to guard Sītā. When Rāma was lured away from the cottage and did not come back for hours, Sītā asked Lakshman to go and look for him. Before Lakshman went to help Rāma, he drew a line on the ground with his bow and warned Sītā not to cross it for any reason. When Lakshman left the cottage, Rāvana, the King of Lankā, appeared, disguised as a religious mendicant, and stood some distance away. Sītā had to cross the line to give him alms, and as she crossed the line Rāvana grabbed hold of her and carried her off to his island kingdom of Lankā. There he kept her in the Ashoka garden, guarded by fierce female demons.

'As Rāma tried to catch the deer, it ran away, so, chasing after it he shot it with an arrow. Suddenly it was transformed into a dead demon. Lakshman saw Rāma kill the demon and both realised that Sītā was in great danger. When they returned, Sītā was missing. Both brothers searched the forest for many months and came to the Southern kingdom of Kishkindhā. Here they met Sugrīva, the deposed king. Rāma made a pact of friendship with Sugrīva and helped him to recover his kingdom from his brother Wāli, while Sugrīva agreed to send his strong and talented monkey general, Hanumān, in search of Sītā. Hanumān found Sītā in the Ashoka garden in Lankā, gave her Rāma's ring as a token of recognition and assured her that Rāma would soon rescue her.

'Hanumān was caught however, and brought before Rāvana who ordered the monkey's tail to be set on fire. As the attendants tied rags to his tail and set them on fire, Hanumān, very cleverly, extended his tail and, jumping from house to house, set fire to most of Rāvana's capital before returning to Rāma.

'Soon Rāma, Lakshman, Sugrīva and Hanumān, with the help of other monkey chiefs like Nala and Nīla, collected a large army and invaded Rāvana's island kingdom, Lankā. There were many battles; Rāvana's brother Kumbha-karna was killed and Lakshman was seriously wounded. Sushena, the physician, needed many medicinal herbs which were only to be found on Mount Gandhamādan. Hanumān went to get the herbs, but, as he could not remember which ones to take, he uprooted the mountain and brought it to Lankā. The physician found the necessary plants and cured Lakshman. Hanumān returned the mountain to its original place.

'In the final battle, Rāma used Indra's dart and killed Rāvana,

Rāma and Sītā, with Hanumān, the Monkey General

Photograph: Ann & Bury Peerless

whose wife Mandodarī mourned her husband. Rāvana's younger brother, Bibhīshana, was placed on the throne of Lankā, and Sītā was united with her husband after many months in captivity. Rāma thanked Sugrīva for his help in rescuing Sītā, and, accompanied by Lakshman and Hanumān, Rāma and Sītā returned to Ayodhyā by means of an aerial car. The people of the capital were happy to welcome their beloved prince, but some expressed doubt about Sītā's purity. To satisfy them, Sītā went through the fire ordeal and, when people saw that Sītā's feet were not burned by the live embers, she was declared pure.

'Soon Rāma's coronation took place and under his wise rule the kingdom prospered and people felt safe. The king's spies were everywhere, gathering people's opinions about Rāma's reputation as king. Most were happy, but one washerman still doubted Sītā's purity. Rāma became disturbed by this gossip about his queen and decided to abandon Sītā, although she was expecting a child, in order to remove suspicion about her. He ordered Lakshman to take her to the hermitage in Vālmiki on the banks of the river Gangā and to leave her there. At Vālmiki's hermitage, *ashram*, Sītā gave birth to twin sons, Kusha and Lawa, who were taught the entire story of Rāma by Vālmiki.

'Some ten years passed and when Rāma performed the *Ashwa-Medha* (Horse Sacrifice) Kusha and Lawa were introduced to their father, and Rāma was united with Sītā. Sītā, however, refused to come to Ayodhyā, saying that if she were pure from the first moment of her captivity to the present day, Mother Earth would break asunder and swallow her then and there. To Rāma's great sorrow, the Earth divided and Sītā disappeared from his life, finally proving her innocence. Stricken with grief and realising his mistake in abandoning Sītā, Rāma gave up his life, and his sons ruled over his kingdom.'

When Ābā finished the story, Tārā and Leenā had tears in their eyes. Gitā, however, was not so moved.

'Ābā,' she said, 'I think Rāma was quite wrong to abandon Sītā after she had performed the fire ordeal, just because some idiot washerman expressed doubt about her purity.'

'But my dear Gitā,' said Ābā, 'Rāma is portrayed as an ideal king and his duties as a king were more important than his duties as a husband. Rāma's behaviour is not for ordinary people.'

'Ābā,' said Tārā, 'I like Hanumān, he is always there to help Rāma.'

'Yes, Tārā, Hanumān is the ideal of a faithful servant. Next week, on the full moon day in the month of *Chaitra*, Hanumān's birth day will be celebrated.'

After the two festivals of New Year's day and Rāma-Navami, the children got down to serious work at school to prepare for their examinations, which were to take place in early April. For Gopāl, Rādhā and Yamū, it meant the extra work of marking papers and writing school reports. They were all looking forward to the school holidays in May, when Vasant would be coming home from Bombay.

2

Avatārs of Vishnu

At last it was *Vaishākh*, the second month in the Hindu calendar, which coincides approximately with May. The annual school examinations were over, and Gopāl and Rādhā were on holiday. The days were beginning to get hot and for about five hours from eleven o'clock in the morning to four in the afternoon the heat was oppressive; hardly anyone went out unless it was absolutely necessary. Wāi is a small town on the bank of the River Krishnā, surrounded by hills and situated on the eastern side of the Western Ghāts, some 20 miles from the hill station 4500 feet high called Mahābaléshwer. The climate is dry, but even in the May to October heat the evenings are cool and pleasant.

Gopāl and Rādhā had come to the river, washed their feet in the cold, clear water and were sitting in the courtyard of one of the Shiva temples, enjoying the cool breeze.

'How old is this temple?' Rādhā asked.

'I think it dates from about 1600. At that time this part of Mahārāshtra was ruled by the Muslim shah of Bijāpur and there used to be a Muslim governor at Wāi. One particular officer named Afzal was a fanatic and he destroyed one old temple dedicated to Ganesha. Legend has it that nothing could be built on the site, and when the Muslims tried to build a mosque there, at least 50 workmen died, so the project was abandoned.'

'But, Gopāl, there is that large Ganesha temple which we can see from here. Why was that not destroyed?' enquired Rādhā.

'Because that Ganesha temple was built about 1761 by a nobleman of the Peshwā, the Hindu ruler of the Marāthās. I am not sure whether it was built on the old site of the temple that was destroyed earlier. This small Shiva temple is interesting because it

The Ganesha Temple in Wāi   *Photograph: V P (Hemant) Kanitkar*

was built in the style invented by Hemādri, the chief minister of the Yādava kings of Deogirī,' said Gōpal.

'In what way is it different?' Rādhā asked as she got up and, removing her sandals, stepped inside the temple. Gopāl followed her and began to explain.

'Look, there is no mortar between the stones; the walls are very thick and the roof is made to taper upwards by putting long stone slabs across the corners of the square. Each succeeding square becomes smaller in size until the onion-shaped dome is built on the top. The spire has plain, quick-lime plaster without any carving or figures.'

'Yes,' said Rādhā, 'it is quite different from other temples.'

Gopāl and Rādhā visited the temple many times during the school holidays, enjoying the cool evening breeze by the river.

On the third day of the month, Govind, in his capacity as priest, visited many houses in the morning and received gifts which he brought home. They included large, unglazed earthen pots, fruit, two *dhotis* and over 100 rupees.

'Uncle Govind, why have you got these pots, bananas and coconuts?' asked Tārā and Leenā, as Govind brought the gifts and put them on the floor in the front room.

'Because this is a day of good luck and people give me gifts in memory of their dead relations so that the coming year will bring them good luck.' As Govind was explaining, Gopāl and Vasant returned from the vegetable market.

'Uncle Gopāl,' said Vasant, 'we need not have bought those bananas and coconuts. Look! My father has received so many gifts today.'

'I was just telling Tārā and Leenā,' said Govind, 'that there are certain days in the year that are auspicious, days when we should make new beginnings, such as starting school, or building a house.'

'Which other days are especially lucky?' asked Leenā.

Now Vasant offered to answer his cousin. 'There is New Year's day.'

'Yes, I remember,' said Tārā, 'when we raised the banner and did that pūjā.'

'That's right,' continued Vasant. 'Then there is the day of *Dasserah* and the day of *Diwali*.'

'But which day of *Diwali*?' Leenā wanted to know. 'Because there are four or five days of *Diwali*.'

'The first day of *Kartik*, that is the fourth day during the festival of *Diwali*,' said Vasant.

'Uncle Govind said today was a good luck day also,' interrupted Tārā.

'Today is lucky only up to mid-day,' Govind said, once again taking charge of the explanation.

'But father,' Vasant addressed Govind, 'why are these days considered auspicious?'

'Because on these days the stars are more favourable and we are more likely to succeed in our work.'

'Does that mean we have only three and a half days in a year which are favourable and other days are against us?'

'No,' said Govind, 'the especially lucky days are set aside for starting particularly big projects.'

Gopāl was taking an interest in the conversation and now he spoke. 'Govind, you went to university; surely you know that stars don't govern our lives completely?'

'Gopāl, I know what you are going to say next: "The fault lies, not in the stars, but in ourselves"—but this is a matter of faith. Hindus are called Star-Gazers, yet the so-called scientific and civilised people in Europe also believe in the influence of planets on man's destiny.'

'Maybe so! Yes, I remember! Neelā, in her last letter from Leicester wrote that many popular newspapers and magazines in Britain print daily and weekly horoscopes of different sun signs. But I am sure the British people don't place as much trust in the stars as we Hindus do in India.'

'True,' said Govind. 'We consult the astrologers more than other experts, but remember, faith begins where logic ends. For me this has been a lucky day.'

Their conversation drew to a close when Ājī came out to ask the girls to go into the kitchen for a snack and invited the men in for their mid-morning cup of tea.

A week later, Ābā, Govind and Gopāl announced that the whole family would visit the temple of Narasimha to celebrate the advent of the deity. Since it was a Sunday when the family outing was discussed, everyone was at home. The four younger children

Avatārs of Vishnu 31

were very keen to attend the nativity festival of the deity and wanted to know many things. Gitā and Ramesh were not entirely ignorant but Tārā and Leenā knew very little.

'Ābā, who is Narasimha?' asked Tārā.

'Well,' said Ābā, 'I had better tell you about the different names of the One God that we worship, then you will know who Narasimha is.

'In our ancient sacred books, called the *Vedas*, this Supreme God is referred to as the Truth. It has no form, and as ordinary people cannot really understand something which they cannot see, the wise men who wrote the *Upanishads*, which are also our sacred texts, thought of another name for the Truth. They said the Supreme God is really *Brahman*. But the ordinary people were still confused and could not understand what Brahman was.'

'So what happened next, Ābā?' asked Leenā.

'Other scholars, who lived after the wise men of the *Upanishads*, took the view that since Brahman created the world, it must be doing three different jobs: creating the world, looking after it and destroying some part of it.'

'I see,' responded Leenā.

'They decided,' continued Ābā, 'to give three different names to Brahman, each one showing one particular side of it.'

'That must be the *Trimūrty*,' said Gītā.

'Yes. The *Trimūrty* consists of *Brahmā*, who makes the world, *Vishnu*, who looks after it and *Shiva*, or *Mahesh*, who destroys a part of it, so that Brahmā can make new things in the world.'

'But who is Narasimha then?' asked Tārā.

'Tell me, Tārā,' said Ābā, 'who looks after the world?'

'Vishnu does. There are so many things Vishnu has to do to protect the world that he has to take on different appearances to do different jobs, or to deal with different dangers.'

'What kinds of dangers?' asked Ramesh.

'Danger from water and danger from wicked men and wild beasts. Vishnu is believed to have appeared on Earth to protect the created world. These appearances are called *Avatārs*; there are ten of them, but the last one is yet to come.'

'I know the first four,' said Gītā.

'Tell us! Tell us!' cried Tārā and Leenā.

'The Fish, the Tortoise, the Boar and Narasimha.'

'Quite right, Gitā,' said Ābā, '*Matsya, Koorma, Varāha* and *Narasimha*, which is half man and half lion.'

'So, Ābā,' said Tārā, 'Narasimha is really Vishnu.'

'Ābā, what comes after Narasimha?' asked Leenā.

'*Vāman*, which means a young boy, and he destroyed a powerful, wicked, but generous king called Bali,' said Ābā. 'Then comes *Parashu-Rāma*, who defeated the warriors who had become arrogant and rude.'

'The next Avatār is *Rāma*,' said Tārā. 'I remember we went to the temple on the day of Rāma-Navami and they gave me that *prasād* made from ginger and sugar. And I burned my tongue.'

'That was because you were greedy and asked for a second helping,' Leenā commented.

'The next Avatār is *Krishna*, followed by *Buddha*. The last one is *Kalki* and is yet to come,' said Ābā, ignoring their squabble.

No one had an opportunity to ask any more questions as Rādhā and Yamū both came to the front room and asked everyone to go into the kitchen for their mid-day meal.

The next morning Govind received a money order for 30 rupees from Mādhav in Delhi. There was a letter from Delhi addressed to Ābā, too. Govind signed the receipt, took the money and the letter, and when the postman had left the house, he gave the letter to Ābā. Ābā opened it and saw that it was from Latā, his daughter, who lived in Delhi with her husband, Mādhav, and their son, Mohan.

> My dear Ābā,
> Mādhav and I fully intended to come to Wāi, with our son, Mohan, for a few days during the May vacation, but unfortunately our leave had to be postponed because two of our colleagues in the library fell ill. Mādhav has sent a money order for 30 rupees, which should arrive at the same time as this letter.
>
> When you take the family for the Narasimha festival, please donate 20 rupees to the temple on our behalf and, using the remaining ten rupees, please send us a coconut by parcel post. It will give us great satisfaction to receive *prasād* from a temple. Perhaps it will only be a substitute, but that coconut *prasād* will bring us good luck. We are all sorry that we cannot be with you for the festival. Mādhav and Mohan are keeping well. My namaskārs (regards) to Ājī, Govind and Gopāl and blessings to

Avatārs of Vishnu 33

the youngsters. We are doing our best to instruct Mohan in the various festivals.

Your affectionate daughter,
Latā

Ābā told the family that Latā and Mādhav would not be able to come to Wāi, and since the festival was only two days away, Gopāl and Govind would have to reserve tickets on the State Transport bus to travel to the temple five miles away.

Then Vasant spoke up: 'Ābā, I don't want to attend the festival.'

'Why not?'

'Because there is nothing new in it. I have seen it all before. It's boring.'

'You are 18 now and you have been doing boring things like eating, wearing clothes, sleeping and taking a bath all your life.'

'But Ābā, that's different. They are necessary for living.'

'Similarly, doing pūjā, celebrating festivals, worshipping God, and believing in some Supreme Force or Spirit is also necessary for living. Without these routine and boring events, as you call them, we would all be mere monkeys, just existing.'

'And there is another important reason,' added Govind, 'why we, as Hindus, should do these boring things.'

'What do you mean, father? What other reason?'

'Look, Vasant, India is a secular state, which means, in theory, that all religions have equal status and full freedom of worship. But lately our Hindu way of life in our own land is coming under great pressure from the followers of other religions. We are all citizens of India, I know, but if we do not preserve our religious traditions, that citizenship will not bring any sense of well-being in our lives. It is up to us to maintain our way of life and preserve our heritage.'

'I did not think about it that way,' said Vasant.

'And another thing,' said Ābā, 'you may not get your cultural identity when you get your degree in commerce in four years time, but you will always have that identity by keeping and practising your Hindu traditions.'

'But there are certain things which I think should be modified or even discontinued,' insisted Vasant.

'Then you must take part in events and try to improve things to suit the needs of the new generation. You will not be able to change certain outdated practices by resigning or opting out.' Ābā continued his argument. 'Look, when laws need changing it is the government in power that has the chance to do so. Mere social reformers do not alter the law by writing about it in newspapers; it is the people in the administration who bring about the necessary changes. That is why you must take part in pūjās and festivals and the rest of it. Now, what do you say?'

'Oh, alright, I will come with you all and take part in the festival,' said Vasant.

'Govind, that means you will have to book 11 return tickets on the bus.'

'Yes, father,' said Govind. And he and Gopāl left for the bus station.

On the afternoon of the festival Ābā took his family to the bus station and passengers began to take up their seats in the special bus that was to travel to the village five miles distant, and bring them back to Wāi after the festival. As the bus left the hard metal roads of the town and travelled along the country road, which was no more than a wide dirt track, a trail of dust, already softened by the narrow, steel tyres of bullock-cart wheels, rose up in its wake, and soon settled on everything near the road.

After a journey lasting half an hour, the bus pulled up in the village square; the passengers got out, dusted their clothes and made their way down rough, stone steps towards the temple near the river. The *mandap* (assembly hall) in front of the shrine was nearly full and Ābā's party made their way inside and sat on the cotton floor covering and began to listen to the priest, who was giving an account of how Vishnu reincarnated himself as Narasimha to save his ardent devotee, Pralhād.

Hiranya Kashipu propitiated Shiva by performing penance. Although he was a notorious demon, Shiva felt that his sincere devotion merited a boon. It is impossible to say what the writer of the myth had in mind. Perhaps he wanted to point out that even a demon had some good in him, and his devotion to Shiva was sincere. Shiva, recognising the merit of the demon duly rewarded it. The story also illustrates the highly developed imagination of the writer.

Hiranya Kashipu wished to be invincible (1) from man or beast; (2) during day or night; (3) inside as well as outside a building; (4) from all known conventional weapons and (5) on Earth, in Water and in the Sky. Vishnu overcame these five conditions of Shiva's boon by (1) appearing not in his usual form, but as half-man, half-lion; (2) at the evening twilight, neither day nor night; (3) on the threshold; (4) using the Lion's claws to kill the demon and (5) by lifting the demon and holding him on his lap (*ie* not on Earth, in Water or in the Sky). The Narasimha story illustrates that God always protects a true devotee from danger and that nothing is impossible to God.

The discourse ended just as darkness fell. People got up and bowed low in the direction of the inner sanctum. After the ārti, many people distributed milksweets and fresh coconut copra and remembered the story from mythology which they had just heard.

On the way back, Govind and Gopāl sat together on the bus and had a serious discussion about the *Avatārs* of Vishnu, as described in the *Puranas*.

'Govind, do you really believe that Vishnu takes on an incarnation to save mankind?' asked Gopāl.

'The stories of various *Avatārs* are recorded in the *Puranas* which are myths and legends. They are to be treated as myths, yet one cannot help admiring the fantastic imagination of the writers of these stories. The Fish incarnation story, in which Manu was saved by the giant fish when there was a great flood, is broadly similar to the Noah legend in Christianity. Rāma and Krishna *Avatārs* are believable incarnations since the *Rāmāyana*, the *Harivamsha* and the *Bhagavadgita* make Rāma and Krishna founders of new orders in Hindu society. And the Buddha is a historical figure. So, yes, I do believe that Vishnu acts as a saviour of mankind when evil abounds in society and traditional values and natural justice are threatened.'

'I am afraid I don't believe Krishna to be a historical figure,' said Gopāl, 'but he is certainly a great teacher and his advice to Arjuna about selfless devotion to duty has moulded the lives of countless millions of Hindus. That reminds me! I think we should teach Tārā and Leenā to recite the *Bhagavadgita*. Don't you agree?'

'Gopāl, they are too young to understand it.'

'I know that, but if they were to learn to read the verses in

Sanskrit, their speech and pronunciation of Marāthī would improve.'

'I agree with you on that point,' said Govind, 'and I suppose I should be the one to start the *Gitā* classes for your daughters.'

'I have a better idea. Why not teach all five children in one go?'

'We'll make a start tomorrow,' said Govind.

'Good. Anyway, going back to our earlier discussion,' Gopāl said, 'I should add that the Avatārs of Vishnu start with the Fish, then comes the Tortoise, which lives on land as well as in the ocean, then comes the Boar, which is a mammal. Narasimha, Vāman and Parashurāma are examples of primitive man. In Rāma we see the beginnings of refinement in man and Krishna is the prototype of modern man. In other words, I think that the *Avatār* concept puts forward a theory to explain how life on Earth evolved.'

Govind gave this a lot of thought. By the time the bus returned to Wāi, Tārā and Leenā were fast asleep and had to be carried into the house by Gopāl and Rādhā.

The following morning Govind asked Vasant, Ramesh and the three girls to come to the front room after their bath. While they were attending to their toilette, Govind performed the morning worship at the household shrine. By the time Govind had finished ārti at the end of the pūjā, the children were ready and waiting for him.

'Why do you want us to sit here, Uncle Govind?' asked Leenā.

'Well, since you have no school for the rest of this month,' began Govind, 'I thought you might like to learn to read the *Bhagavadgitā*.'

'Yes, we both would like that,' said Tārā, 'but we have no book of the *Gitā*.'

'We can buy some copies in a few days time, but today I shall use the large copy which we keep in the shrine. All you have to do is to learn the correct way of saying Sanskrit words. It will be difficult at first, but you will get the hang of it soon. Are you ready?'

When all five were ready, Govind told them that the *Gitā* was preached by Shri Krishna to Arjuna on the battlefield of Kuru-Kshetra, when the sons of Pandu were about to fight their cousins, the Kuru princes, for their rightful share in the kingdom.

Then he began to say the first verse very slowly and asked them to repeat the words after him.

'*Dharma Kshetre. Kuru-Kshetre. Samavetā. Yuyutsavah.*'

The older children found little difficulty but Tārā and Leenā had to be coached even more slowly before they were able to recite the first line: '*Mamakah . . . Pandavaschaiva . . . Kim akurvata Sanjaya.*'

After half an hour, the children had learned to read six verses. Govind felt very pleased that they had made a good beginning. As the month drew to a close the children learned chapters 1 and 15 off by heart. It was also time for Vasant to think about returning to Bombay to start his second year at Poatdār College of Commerce.

3

Praise of Gangā, River Worship, Mahābhārata

It was the seventh day of *Jyeshtha*, the third month of the Hindu year. The schools had reopened after the holidays and Gopāl, Rādhā, Ramesh and the three girls were the first to get ready in the morning, followed by Govind, who had six pūjās to perform in the houses of his patrons. Ābā was the last to take a bath; while bathing he was in the habit of reciting Sanskrit verses in praise of Vishnu, Shiva, the Trimūrty, Ganesha and the presiding spirits of holy lakes and rivers, particularly the River Ganges. He had been doing this all his life since his thread ceremony and, although he was over 1000 miles from the holy Ganges, he invoked the river deity to be present in the water he used for his bath. The following translations express Ābā's faith:

1 'I bow to Vishnu, the Lord of the Universe, the dispeller of fear from the living, the object of meditation of the Yogins, the Lotus-eyed, the husband of Laxmi, the supporter of the world, infinite as the sky, having a heavenly body the colour of the clouds, the Lord of Gods, with a lotus in his navel, possessing a serene form and reclining on the coils of Shesha serpent.'

2 'Victory to you, Oh Great God Shambhu, the ocean of compassion! Forgive my transgressions committed through the actions of my body, hands, feet, tongue, ears, eyes and mind, which may have been prescribed or prohibited by the codes of good conduct.'

3 'I bow before my Guru and mentor, for he is like Brahmā, Vishnu and Shiva; indeed he is the Supreme Spirit, Brahman, made manifest.'

4 'Salutation before any god ultimately reaches *Keshava*

(Vishnu), in the same way that the rain water finally reaches the ocean.'

5 'I bow before Ganesha, the Lord of the Ganas, the remover of all obstacles, who is worshipped by the Gods and the demons for the fulfilment of their supplications.'

6 'May the rivers (the Goddesses) Gangā, Sindhu, Saraswatī, Yamunā, Godāvarī and Narmadā, Kāveri, Sharayū, Mahendra Tanayā, Charmanvatī, Vedikā, Kshiprā, Vetravatī and Mahāsuranadī (also called Gandakī) who are filled with pure waters, along with the ocean, bring us good fortune.'

7 'Oh presiding goddesses of the rivers Gangā, Yamunā, Godāvarī, Saraswatī, Narmadā, Sindhu and Kāveri, purify this water by your divine presence.'

8 'I bow before you, Oh Mother Ganges, possessing lotus-like feet and divine form honoured by Gods and Demons alike. You grant a good life and release from the cycle of birth and death always according to men's devotion.'

9 'Whosoever, although hundreds of miles away from the holy river, utters the words "Gangā, Oh, Gangā," is forgiven all transgressions and sins of omission and reaches Vishnu's abode.'

10 'You are the Sovereign of all holy waters, you are indeed the Origin of the World. I bow before you so that you may graciously grant my supplications.'

11 'May the presiding spirits of the holy waters like Lake Pushkara and the holy rivers like Gangā always sanctify my bath water with their divine presence.'

12 'I am sin incarnate, I commit sins, my soul is tainted and I have been born out of sin. Protect me by your compassion, Oh Mother Ganges, and wash away all my sins.'

After Ābā had finished his bath he put on a clean cotton dhoti and shirt and sat in the small household shrine for a few minutes silently meditating and praying for the continued well-being of his family.

Yamū and Ājī were in the kitchen, cleaning and cutting vegetables, and sifting out grit from rice and lentils for their mid-day meal. Ājī left Yamū to start the preparation of various items for lunch and, going near the shrine, asked Ābā whether he would like a cup of tea.

'Yes, that would be nice. Bring it to the front room', he said. In the front room he sat on the thick cotton cloth on the floor and started reading a Marāthī newspaper which Gopāl had bought early that morning.

When Ājī brought him a cup of tea, Ābā did not express his thanks by words but looked at his wife with a look of tender affection and gratitude. Slightly nodding his head, he smiled in appreciation.

'I have put three spoonfuls of sugar in your tea,' said Ājī, as she went back to the kitchen, leaving Ābā to his newspaper.

Govind returned from his morning round of visiting his patrons' houses to perform pūjās. When he came home, Yamū simply came to the door of the front room that separated that room from the middle room, looked at her husband and, without saying anything, went back to her work. She did not speak to her husband in the presence of her father-in-law, even although she was a well-educated woman and Ābā was not very orthodox in his relations towards his two daughters-in-law. Yet in middle-class, high caste Hindu families, the younger couples do not hold long conversations in the presence of their elders.

'There is the river worship festival this week and it is our turn to do pūjā and prepare *prasād* tonight,' Govind said to Ābā, loudly enough for Yamū to hear. Ājī came out to the front room, followed by Yamū, who stood in the doorway.

'What shall we prepare for *prasād*?' Govind asked Ājī, questioning Yamū, his wife, with his eyes.

'Why not prepare some spiced red beans!' interjected Ābā, putting down his paper and looking at Ājī and Yamū.

'We have two kilos of beans,' said Yamū. 'I will go and soak them in hot water. They will be ready to be cooked by this evening.'

When Ājī had gone back to the kitchen, Ābā spoke. 'I think we need to educate our people here, in public health. People throw their rubbish into the streets, and many use the same streets as public toilets.'

'It is a lost cause, Ābā,' said Govind, 'for two reasons: not many towns have public conveniences; and of course, in villages, no such thing exists. Also, people just do not have any understanding. They only know of their personal cleanliness. Our towns and cities are a disgrace.'

Community activities at the River Godavari, Nasik Photograph: *V P (Hemant) Kanitkar*

'That is why our children need to be trained to be citizens, not just degree holders,' said Ābā. 'We have sublime ideas about God and the soul and *Moksha* (the release from the cycle of birth and death) but in reality we have to live in dirty surroundings.'

After lunch, Govind went out with a bucket to the river and, with the help of four other people, washed the long stone steps built near the river. When he returned he felt that he had done his public service for the day. 'At least the stone steps near the river are clean, even if the area further downstream is filthy,' he said to Ābā.

When the girls came home, followed by Ramesh, they were told that after an early evening meal they could go to the river with Govind, Ābā and Gopāl for pūjā and prasād that evening. 'You can prepare some lamps to float in the water at the time of pūjā,' said Ābā and promptly took out four bowls made of dried banyan leaves from a cupboard in the middle room. Āji prepared four thick cotton wicks with a wide base and soaked them in ghee (clarified butter). She asked Gitā to stand the wicks upright in the leaf bowls and pour some thick ghee into each bowl as additional fuel.

After their evening meal, Ābā, his two sons and four grandchildren, went to the river. Gitā, Tārā and Leenā carried the leaf-bowl lamps, Govind took the pūjā equipment, and Ramesh carried a large brass saucepan of spiced red beans which Yamū had cooked earlier. As Govind performed the pūjā, many children lit their lamps and floated them in the water. The gentle current began to take the floating lamps downstream as Govind and seven other men did the ārti. One boy splashed water into Leenā's lamp and drowned it. Leenā started to cry, but Gitā managed to persuade her that it was only an accident and that the boy did not mean to drown her lamp. Leenā soon forgot the incident as she took prasād from Ramesh. The spiced beans were served straight onto open hands and everyone enjoyed them. They had to climb down the steps to the water's edge to wash their hands. There must have been about 50 people attending this pūjā of the river deity, but only two or three were able to look beyond blind faith.

A few days later there was a special lecture arranged at the public library to commemorate the 312th anniversary of Shivāji's Coronation and, although many prominent residents of the town were invited, only Hindus turned up for the meeting. A Professor of History from Poona was the chief guest. He was a well-known scholar, and although he was not born into the Brahmin *Varna* (class), through his clear intellect and profound learning he had achieved the social status of a traditional Brahmin and was respected by them. Of course, there were some orthodox members of the priestly class who would not have even dreamed of inviting the learned professor into their homes for a meal, for eating together is a true test of breaking down the *Varna* or *Jati* barrier. Ābā had worked in the civil court all his life and had met people from different levels of society in his official capacity as a head clerk; this had taught him to treat people on their merits and most of the time he did not think of a person's caste. Occasionally, however, he became aware of it if an educated, well-dressed and well-spoken person behaved in a manner which belied his outward appearance.

Ābā and Gopāl went to the public library and as they entered the first floor assembly hall they were greeted by the Librarian and shown to the vacant chairs towards the back of the hall. Ābā noticed that there were doctors, lawyers, priests, shopkeepers, teachers from the Boys' High School, some women teachers from the Girls' High School, and some men who worked as clerks in the civil court, the State Transport bus station, the Urban Co-operative Bank and the State Bank. There were no Muslims or Christians in the hall although there were prominent and well-to-do people from those religious groups who lived and worked in the town.

When Professor Mohite arrived, everyone in the hall rose to their feet and after the guest had taken his seat, they also sat down. After a brief speech of welcome by the sub-judge of the town, the learned professor began:

'Ladies and Gentlemen, I am not going to recite the detailed chronological history of Shivājī which you all know, but will mention only the important objectives in his career of some 35 years. In that short active life, he established a Hindu kingdom in this part of India, which gave freedom of worship to all his subjects according to their faith, and he made the Marāthās into a hard-working and self-reliant people.

'Shivājī was born in 1627 to Jijābāi, a princess from the Jādhav family who was married to Shahji Bhoslé, the son of a humble headman of a village who became a prominent soldier at the court of Ahamadnagar, through his resourcefulness and enterprise. When Shahji joined the kingdom of Bijāpur, after the demise of Ahamadnagar, he was granted private estates near Poona. Shivājī inherited these estates and with his mother's encouragement began to carve out a kingdom for himself, but his main aim was to achieve political independence so that Hindus would be able to worship God according to their faith and without any interference from the Muslim rulers of Bijāpur, Golkonda and Delhi. After a series of victories against Muslim armies, his kingdom began to grow in size, until it covered the whole of the Marāthā country by 1674. Although he wanted freedom of worship for Hindus, he never denied it to Muslims and made grants to Hindu temples as well as shrines of Muslim *Pirs* (saints).

'He employed people from all caste groups and gave them jobs to enable them to increase their merit in different ways. Brahmins were priests and clerks as well as soldiers and keepers of forts, the warrior class were fittingly employed as commanders of armies and garrisons and as common soldiers. Members of lower castes were employed according to their merit. Muslims worked in

Shivāji's navy and Mullah Haider was his trusted envoy employed in negotiations with Muslim Sultans. No caste group was given any special privileges. This meant that everyone's talents were utilised in the service of the state.

'I am now going to say something about the present position; the employment and educational opportunities that are reserved for the "scheduled castes". When our country became independent in 1947, there were few opportunities for the lower castes in our society. The central and state governments devised special laws which reserved places in educational institutions for the "scheduled castes" and also jobs in the various departments of the administration.

'This positive attitude improved the educational and social level of the lower castes, but when the time limit, which was 15 years to begin with, was increased yet again, the reserved places were not always filled with people of the right calibre. A kind of false security has led to the lowering of standards in many cases. Talented children from high caste families are often denied admission to colleges because of the reserved places for "scheduled castes". Often talent is wasted and many Indians, many Hindus, with enterprise, have left our country to settle and work abroad. Untouchability was abolished by law when India became a Republic, but the "reserved" places and jobs have, in fact, kept caste consciousness alive.

'We have gathered here to remember Shivāji's work, but we have forgotten to utilise people's merit, and have established a "privileged group" which is not getting the competition so essential for improvement. What we need is opportunity for all sections of society based on healthy competition. That will be a true memorial to Shivāji.'

When Professor Mohite sat down, a window behind him was shattered by a stone thrown by someone outside the library. There was a sudden commotion, but the professor got up, asking people to sit down again. 'What you see behind me is reminiscent of the work of another privileged group in our society. Muslims have indulged in stone-throwing activities at Hindu festivals and Yātras, and, last year, at Nasik and Panwel, processions on Shivāji's birthday were stoned by them, causing injuries. When Muslims do such things, they are said to be protecting their religious rights, but when Hindus retaliate, we are promptly labelled "communal, right-wing, Hindu fanatics". That is the price we have to pay for having a secular state.'

The lecture certainly caused a minor sensation in the town.

When Ābā and Gopāl returned home, they found Govind making preparations for the Banyan tree worship—pūjā—which was to take place in two days time.

The Banyan tree worship is a part of popular Hinduism, and it is linked with the Sāvitri story contained in the *Mahābhārata*. This religious observance is limited to middle-class Hindu married women whose husbands are living. It is diffiicult to perform this pūjā in large cities, as few banyan trees can survive there. This is because the banyan tree expands rapidly by sprouting new roots from its branches which support the main trunk, forming a series of lesser trunks. As space is at a premium in the built up areas of a city, banyan trees flourish better in country areas. The banyan tree is to the Indian subcontinent what the oak is to Europe; it is very long-lived.

The day before the Full Moon day in the third month of the Hindu year, married women gather near the chosen tree and wind cotton thread around its trunk and pour water at its base. On the Full Moon day, after their morning bath, they perform pūjā which a priest directs, reciting appropriate mantras. Women pray for a long married life and commemorate Sāvitri and Satyawān as the ideal of conjugal love and fidelity. A complete fast is observed during the day and it is broken after sunset. The following day, gifts of a sari, a coconut, rice grains tinged with kum-kum (red powder) and half a dozen bangles, the symbols of a woman's marital status, are given to the priest and his wife.

Ājī, Yamū and Rādhā performed the banyan tree pūjā and the three girls went along to observe how it was done. When they came back, Gita wanted to know why a tree was offered worship.

'Ābā, will you tell us how the banyan tree is connected with the Sāvitri story and where the story comes from?'

'I think your father is better qualified to tell you the origin of the story and what happened to Sāvitri,' replied Ābā. 'After all, he is a priest.'

When Govind began to explain the story after lunch, Ājī, Yamū and Rādhā joined the three girls, almost as a pious duty.

'Since the Sāvitri story is found in the *Mahābhārata*,' Govind began, 'I shall tell you something about that poem first before I go on to the story of Sāvitri and Satyawān. The *Mahābhārata*, as it exists today, is the longest single poem in the world; it has 100 000 verses. The main story concerns the struggle between the Kuru princes and their cousins, the five sons of Pandu, over a kingdom situated in the fertile land north of Delhi.

'Although Dhritarāshtra, the father of the Kuru princes, was older than Pandu, his brother, he was deemed not eligible to rule because he was blind. Pandu would have inherited the kingship had he been alive, but since he had died earlier, his eldest son, Yudhisthir, became entitled to rule. The sons of Dhritarāshtra were not willing to acknowledge the claim of their cousin. However, the kingdom was divided equally by the blind uncle; the Kuru princes ruled their half from Hastināpur while the sons of Pandu established their capital at Indraprastha. The sons of Dhritarāshtra wanted the whole kingdom, so they challenged their cousins to a gambling match. The Kuru princes won everything from their cousins, with the help of Shakuni, a wicked uncle, who used loaded dice.

'The sons of Pandu were promised that their half of the kingdom would be restored to them after they had lived in exile for 13 years, the last of which had to be spent incognito. The Pandu princes fulfilled their side of the bargain and at the end of the thirteenth year of their exile, appeared before their cousins at Hastināpur and demanded their half of the kingdom. The Kuru princes refused to recognise their cousins' claim, so the sons of Pandu declared war on the sons of Dhritarāshtra. The great battle was fought for 18 days at Kuru-Kshetra, and the Kuru princes and their vast army were totally destroyed. And so, the sons of Pandu ruled peacefully for a long time over the entire kingdom.

'The original version of the *Mahābhārata* dealt only with the feud between the cousins, but various writers during successive centuries added different episodes in appropriate places until all the tribes of the sub-continent came to be included in the poem. The traditional author of the *Mahābhārata* is Vyāsa, a Brahmin poet, but in its present form the epic is not the work of a single person. There are 18 cantos in this epic and the Sāvitri story occurs in one of those. The *Bhagavadgitā* is also part of this epic poem and appears as Krishna's advice to Arjuna about his *dharma*—moral duty. Now listen to the story of Sāvitri and Satyawān.

'Long, long ago in ancient India there was a rich and powerful king called Ashwapati who had a beautiful daughter named Sāvitri. When the princess reached the age of marriage, many young and handsome princes sought her hand. At the same time, the royal priests informed the king of one particular prince called Satyawān. He was young and handsome, and certainly a prince of the royal blood. But alas, he had no kingdom. His father had been defeated in a battle, the kingdom overrun by the enemy, and, into the bargain, he had become blind. Satyawān his son had to accept this cruel turn of fate and he retired to the forest with his parents to live a simple life. When the princess learned all about the unfortunate prince, she decided to marry him. When she told her father of her resolve, the king was surprised, to say the least. He tried to persuade her to marry some other prince. The king could not understand why Sāvitri chose this penniless man. As time went on, the princess became more and more determined and, at last, the king gave his consent so that she could marry the man of her choice. The princess gave up her life of luxury and comfort, put on a simple sari and, taking just a few clothes, went to the forest where Satyawān took care of his blind father and his grief-stricken mother. The princess married her prince in a simple ceremony, and was very happy. Her most cherished dream had come true.

'She devoted herself entirely to the welfare of her parents-in-law and her husband. However, before the princess married Satyawān, she was told that the prince had only one year to live. She had not taken this seriously. But now that she lived in a forest, away from the round of pleasures in the palace, she had time on her hands, and she began to count the days of her husband's remaining life. She tried to remain cheerful, hiding her secret worry. As time passed, she became anxious about her prince.

'One day when they were walking in the woods, Satyawān felt very tired and lay down beneath a large banyan tree. The princess sat near him, supporting his head in her lap. As her husband became unconscious, she realised that the year was over and it was the day when he would die. Deep in her thoughts she became aware of the presence of some being. Then she saw a figure mounted on a large buffalo and holding a rope in his hands. It was the Spirit of Death. She spoke of her love for her husband. She pleaded with the Spirit of Death for her husband's life, but Death remained unmoved. She continued to speak and finally convinced Death that she loved her husband.

' "I understand how you feel about your husband," said Death, "but my plans cannot be altered. Ask for anything except your husband's life and I will grant your request."

'The princess rose to her feet and bowed before Death with deep respect before she spoke.

' "I ask for nothing for myself," she said, "but please let my father-in-law *see* his grandson safely seated on the throne of his former kingdom."

'The Spirit of Death, moved by this selfless request, gazed long and thoughtfully at the princess, then gave his consent. The princess bowed again in gratitude. The bargain was complete. The Spirit of Death smiled at the cleverness of the princess, withdrew his snares and left empty-handed. Satyawān woke from his deep sleep and could not understand why Sāvitri had tears in her eyes. They were tears of triumph over Death. By her request she had got back her father-in-law's sight, his former kingdom, and her husband's life, for she would have to bear a son if the promise were to be fulfilled.'

When Govind had finished the story, Tārā asked him whether all women in India did the banyan tree pūjā.

'No, Tārā, only married Hindu women whose husbands are living. Even then, not all Hindu women do this pūjā because they probably do pūjās in other parts of India which we don't do here.'

Yamū and Rādhā got up to make tea and the special religious observance was nearly over. Since there were no special religious days for the rest of the month, the secular pattern of life of the Wāiker family was not disturbed. The month was nearly over and the Monsoons had started with full force.

4

Pilgrimage, Varna and Jāti, Karma

As the month of *Āshādh*, the fourth month in the Hindu calendar, opened, Ābā had a visit from one of his neighbours, Rāmji, who belonged to the artisan caste and worked as a carpenter.

'Raam-raam, Ābāji,' said Rāmji, as he came through the front door. Crossing the small courtyard, he climbed the two stone steps and sat on the edge of the floor-covering where Ābā was sitting, reading a Marāthi newspaper after his bath. His three granddaughters and Ramesh, Govind's son, were in the middle room, finishing their homework and sorting out books that were needed in school that day. Govind was performing the morning pūjā in the household shrine; Gopāl and Rādhā were getting ready for school, while Ājī and Yamū were in the kitchen, preparing vegetables and planning the mid-day meal.

'Raam-raam, Rāmji.' Ābā returned the greeting. 'Have you finished making the door for the new house of the flour-mill owner?'

'Yes, only yesterday. I shall not be able to take on any more work for a little while, but we shall manage on our savings,' said Rāmji.

'Why is that? Are you not well?' enquired Ābā.

'By the grace of Pānduranga, I am in good health. But I shall be going on the first of the bi-annual pilgrimages to Pandharpūr.'

'Oh, I forgot that the eleventh day of this month is very important for men of God like you, Rāmji.'

'You are also a man of God, Ābāji, but you do not care to go on a pilgrimage.'

'Rāmji, I offer worship to Him in my house or in the temple, for He is everywhere.'

'Indeed, He is everywhere, Ābāji, but a particular shrine at a

The Vithobā Temple in Pandharpūr Photograph: *V P (Hemant) Kanitkar*

particular place has its own charm. That is why you should try to walk to Pandharpūr this year with our party. There will be about 20 of us in the group, including some women.'

'I think I can manage to walk the 140 miles to reach the town, but I don't think I can accept the filthy surroundings when we get there. Do we have to leave so much rubbish in that pilgrimage centre to prove our devotion to Vithobā?'

As Ābā mentioned the fact of the filthy atmosphere of the holy place, Rāmji tried to use it in his argument, to persuade Ābā to join the pilgrimage. 'If you don't like the filth, Ābāji, why not join us and try to educate the pilgrims to be more careful? You see, Ābā, most of them don't even think about the surroundings when they get there; they are only concerned with visiting the temple and touching the feet of the Vithobā image.'

'That is all very well, but when non-Hindus visit the place they are unable to perceive the devotion. All they can see is the dirt and human refuse in the streets; they are shocked and disgusted. The devout Hindus do not even seem to see the dirt as they stand in the long queues waiting for a chance to have Darshan of Vithobā,' said Ābā with genuine concern.

('Darshan' means 'viewing' the image in the inner sanctum of a temple from the doorway. It is not always possible for people to enter the inner sanctum of a temple, particularly at the time of the festival when many thousands will be waiting in the queue.)

'Ābāji, we need people like you among the pilgrims to teach them to behave with cleanliness as well as devotion. On the other hand there are no adequate facilities for good sanitation and the poor villagers don't know how to behave.'

'Tell me, Rāmji, how long will it take you to reach Pandharpūr?'

'About nine or ten days. We are sometimes lucky enough to get a lift in a bullock-cart or even a seat on a bus. Why? Are you thinking of joining our party this year?'

'I shall have to discuss the matter with Ājī and Govind.'

'Does a man need the permission of his wife and son to visit Lord Vithobā? Make up your own mind, Ābāji; let God look after other matters. Once you get there, you will be so deep in the river of devotion you will not have time to think of anything else, not even the dirty surroundings. You will not think of anyone's caste, and you will forget that you are a Brahmin and I am a carpenter. We shall be children of Vithobā.'

Ābā called Ājī and asked her to make a cup of tea for Rāmji. It was Yamū who brought two cups of tea to the front room. Ābā gave one cup to Rāmji and took the other himself. As they drank tea, Ābā decided to go on the pilgrimage. He had never thought before of walking the long distance to Pandharpūr and visiting the shrine of Vithobā, which is another name of Vishnu. As the two men finished their tea, Govind came out to the front room and greeted Rāmji.

'Raam-raam, Rāmji.'

'Raam-raam, Govindrāo.'

'When will you be going to Pandharpūr?' asked Govind, when he heard Rāmji's news.

'We start tomorrow evening. I was just asking Ābāji to join our group this year. I think it will be a new experience for him to meet Hindus of different castes, forgetting their high or low places in their villages and towns and becoming equal children of God for a few days.' Rāmji tried to persuade Ābā in a roundabout way.

'I think Rāmji is right,' said Ābā, 'I will go on the pilgrimage for the first time. Since I have retired, it is the right time of life for me to experience such things. My sons and their wives will look after the house and take care of Ājī for a few days.'

'Do not worry about things here, Ābā,' said Govind. 'We shall take care of everything.'

'We start tomorrow evening, Ābāji,' said Rāmji, as he left the Wāiker house.

Ājī and Yamū prepared 30 chapatis and dry vegetable curry and also some *lādoos* (sweets) for Ābā to take with him. Ābā took three dhotis and shirts, a light cotton blanket and a rough woollen blanket with him. Taking Govind's advice, he took 60 rupees for food, and tea and sugar for the journey. The next evening Ābā, joined by Rāmji, met other members of the party, and as they walked away from Wāi along the road to Pandharpūr, he felt quite elated by this new experience.

Now that Ābā had gone on pilgrimage, Govind, being the eldest male in the family, was temporarily head of the household. On the tenth day of the month, Govind asked Gitā, Tārā and Leenā to

Lord Vishnu resting on the coils of the Shesha serpent
Photograph: Ann & Bury Peerless

come and sit on the rough cotton floor-covering in the front room, so that he could explain to them the special religious observances that are kept in the four-month period between the eleventh day of *Āshādh* and the eleventh day of *Kārtik*, the eighth month of the Hindu calendar.

'Gitā, do you know what is meant by *chaturmās?*'

'Yes, father, it means four months.'

'But which four months?' Govind asked. Gitā was unsure, so he continued: 'The four-month period between the eleventh day of Āshādh and the eleventh day of Kārtik.'

'Ājī was saying tomorrow is a fasting day,' said Tārā.

'That's right. Chaturmās begins tomorrow,' said Govind.

'But Uncle,' asked Leenā, 'what is so special about chaturmās?'

'Well, in the *Purānas* we are told that Lord Vishnu enjoys complete rest from his responsibility of looking after the world. He sleeps on the coils of the Shesha serpent for four months, during which time men and women need to take more care over their lives. The various religious days, such as fasting days, are designed to regulate our lives.'

'Who observes the fasting days and why?' asked Gitā.

'During the Monsoon period, when the air is damp, we are not able to digest certain foods, so, many people give up eating heavy food. Some men and most women observe a complete fast on certain days, but if a complete fast is not possible then some light and nourishing foods are allowed. Women do heavy work, not only in the home but in the fields as well, so they need a periodic supply of nourishing food, which is allowed on fasting days. That is why most women observe a fast on certain days. They also believe that they will gain *Punya*—religious merit—which will bring happiness for the whole family.'

'How do women start these observances?' asked Gitā.

'Before the start of an observance, women offer prayers to the family deity, saying which observance they intend to keep and asking for blessing and strength to complete the undertaking. During the period of the observance they should forgive others for their mistakes, speak the truth, show kindness to everyone and keep the house very clean, offering hospitality to all guests. Some women fast on Mondays to worship Shiva, on Saturdays to worship Hanumān, on Tuesdays to worship Pārvati; in fact on any particular day to worship the main family deity, such as Vishnu.'

'Uncle Govind, what happens after the four months?'

'When the observance is completed successfully, friends and relations are invited for a feast and certain gifts are given to the family priest.'

'Can we do anything special during chaturmās, or are we too young?' asked Leenā.

'I don't think you should do any fasting. Why don't you make a promise to yourself that you will study much harder for the next four months. That will be as good as any observance your mother or Gitā's mother might decide to undertake.'

Govind's suggestion was received with enthusiasm by Gitā, Tārā and Leenā, and they looked forward to the important fasting day. The next day, being the start of chaturmās, Ājī, Yamū and Rādhā prepared fasting day food for everyone. They cooked previously-soaked sago with ghee, and jirā seeds with a little salt and a pinch of red chilli powder, a thin, soup-like curry of crushed peanuts; and thin fried potato slices in ghee. In addition, they had dates, bananas and a soft toffee of fresh coconut and sugar.

As Govind said grace in Sanskrit before their mid-day meal, Ājī silently prayed to Vithobā to enable Ābā to have his *Darshan* at the temple in Pandharpūr. Gitā wanted to know what Ājī, Yamū and Rādhā were going to observe during chaturmās.

Ājī said that she was going to perform a silent prayer, repeating a twelve letter formula—'*Om Na Mo Bha ga va te Vā su de Vā ya*'—a thousand times every day. Yamū and Rādhā had decided to give up eating rice for four months. Tārā said that Gitā, Leenā and herself would study hard. Govind, being a practising priest, would have to give up onion and garlic, and Ramesh was going to try to learn all 700 verses of the *Bhagavadgitā* off by heart.

In actual fact, the various observances undertaken by different members of the Waiker family may not be practised by Hindus in other regions of India. Different areas have different foci of religious practice, since not all families worship the Supreme Spirit—Brahman—through the same personification. Broadly speaking, Hindus may be divided into three categories: those worshipping Vishnu; those devoted to Shiva; and those who honour the Mother Goddess, Pārvati (or Shakti) the female energy in Creation.

Most Hindus hold the *Vedas* to be sacred revelations; subscribe to the theory of the reincarnation of *Ātman*—the soul—which is born again and again in different bodies as a result of one's *Karma*, which is the sum total effect of one's actions; and accept the main message of the *Bhagavadgitā*, namely, that one must act in life with a selfless detachment, according to one's *Dharma*—or moral duty—which is determined by one's age, education, social position and occupation.

The most important concept which governs Hindu belief and practice is *Dharma*, which permeates the whole society in four ways: namely, *Varna Dharma*, applicable to the entire *Varna* (social class or category); *Ashrama Dharma*, applicable to every individual at each stage of their lives, the *Ashramas* being the student stage of life, the householder stage, the retirement stage and, finally, the renouncement of worldly responsibility stage; *Kula Dharma*, the duties laid down by one's family tradition; and, finally, *Jāti Dharma*, the duties of one's caste determined by one's occupation. There are no apparent rights for any Hindu, because each person's rights are embodied in others' duties.

Traditionally the ancient Aryan settlers in India divided their society into four *varnas*—classes or categories—which were:

Brahmins—priests and professionals;
Kshtriyas—warriors, administrators and rulers;
Vaishyas—merchants and cultivators of land and livestock; and
Shudras—artisans, such as potters, basket weavers and metal workers.

A fifth group, which may have been composed of the conquered original inhabitants of India, was assigned all the dirty jobs for the upper varnas. The unclean nature of the work done by people such as leather workers and removers of dead cattle, debased their social position to such a low level that their physical touch was abhorred and sometimes even their shadows were shunned. Hence they are known by the name 'untouchables'.

In the early stages, varna and jāti rank was based on ability and function, and there was a great deal of social mobility since occupations were not, as yet, determined by birth. As vested interests grew, birth and family determined jāti and the whole society became stratified into a rigid monolithic system in which the higher castes, even though lacking in merit, claimed a superior social and ritual position. Sons began to follow their fathers' hereditary occupations and were not allowed to change, because of strict caste rules, jealousies and taboos. The lot of the untouchables has not improved greatly in this century, although Mahātma Gandhi gave them a new name, 'Harijans', the children of God.

For the Wāiker family nothing of consequence happened until Ābā returned from his pilgrimage to the Vithobā (Vishnu) shrine at Pandharpūr on the twenty-third day of the month. As it was a Sunday, everyone was at home, and after Ābā had had a bath and offered a prayer of thanks to the family deities for his safe return, Ājī and Yamū made tea for everyone and brought it to the front room where they all had gathered.

'Ābā, did you find the long walk difficult? Was it hard to find food and overnight accommodation during your journey?' Gopāl was concerned about how his father had coped with the strain.

'Well!' Ābā began. 'As we walked away from Wāi, I was doubtful whether I would be able to cover the distance of 140 miles on foot, but we walked at a steady pace, singing the traditional songs of devotion, and after about six hours we stopped for food and rest in a small village. I may say I felt tired then, but after taking some chapatis and hot tea, I felt refreshed. We rested for about four hours and then continued our walk. That was the regular pattern; walking for six hours and then resting for about four or five. We found a place to sleep in different villages and people were very helpful. After two days, walking became less tiring and as our goal came nearer our enthusiasm increased. We reached Pandharpūr the day before the main festival of Darshan and immediately joined the mile-long queue.'

'How many pilgrims had gathered there?' asked Govind.

'I am sure there were at least three *lakhs*, which is about 300 000. I had a friend who went to Pandharpūr many years ago when the priests were in complete charge of the temple and he had to pay 100 rupees to view the image in the inner sanctum. There was a lot of mismanagement and poor people were robbed by the priests. But a few years ago, the State government sacked the priests and took over the management of the temple. We did not have to pay more than ten rupees each and there was a lot of discipline enforced by the police. Absolutely no one missed the *Darshan* and I noticed little filth in the town. However, as soon as we had viewed the image, we decided to leave the town and went to a small hamlet, about three miles distant. There we bathed in the river and spent three rupees each for a meal. That night we rested in a *dharmashālā*—an alms house—and started our return journey the next day.'

'Was Rāmji right about everyone feeling equal before God?' asked Govind.

'Yes. There were people from all walks of life; there were lecturers from colleges in Poona, doctors, teachers, farmers, potters and leather workers. They did not think about their castes; they were all devotees of Vithobā. Do you know, I ate a chapati given to me by a farmer, a thing I would not have done in Wāi. As Hindus we have complete freedom to worship any deity of our choice and we normally offer worship as individuals. At Pandharpūr, people offered worship as a group and this must be one of the few instances of congregational worship in our faith.'

'Ābā,' Tārā said, 'what have you brought for us from Pandharpūr?'

Ābā opened his cloth shopping bag and took out a packet containing roasted chickpeas and discs of boiled sugar. He also took out a string of prayer beads which he wore round his neck.

'I have brought prasād—blessed offering—from Pandharpūr,' he said and distributed the prasād. As they received it, each person bent down and touched Ābā's feet in honour of his having returned from a pilgrimage. Ājī and Govind were of one opinion that Ābā had gained much religious merit from his pilgrimage.

Towards the end of that month, Ābā had a visitor who shocked and surprised him by his appearance. Ābā had just finished his morning prayers and was in the front room having a cup of tea when Keshar walked through the front door and, crossing the courtyard, came and sat on the stone steps leading to the front room.

'Namaskār, Ābā.'

'Namaskār,' said Ābā, not recognising the visitor. As Keshar sat on the steps and looked silently at Ābā, he presented a pathetic figure. He was nearly 40 years old, his natural fair skin looked weather-beaten, his hair was unkempt and growing wildly on his head. His eyes were bloodshot and his week-old stubble covered his face like black emery paper. His shirt and loose pyjama trousers were grubby, streaked with dust and sweat, and he wore nothing on his feet.

'You look familiar but I can't place you; neither can I remember your name,' said Ābā.

'I am Keshar; I live in the next street.'

'Oh, Keshar! You have changed since I saw you six or seven months ago. What has happened? Why are you in this condition?'

'It is my *Karma*,' replied Keshar, touching his forehead with the palm of his right hand.

'You are talking rubbish, you don't seem to know the meaning of the word Karma.'

'I know what Karma is. It is fate, it is Kismet,' replied Keshar.

'That is quite wrong. People who have to live in grinding poverty, who are without basic education and have little or no opportunity to improve the quality of their lives, may be excused if they blame their condition on their fate or Karma. They are caught in the web of life like helpless flies; they are drowning in the flood of circumstances, clutching at the straw of Karma.' Ābā spoke very seriously, hoping to help Keshar.

'But it is my Karma,' said Keshar.

'Well, let us consider your Karma. Your parents were rich and kind and they gave you and your brother a good education. You never starved, on the contrary, you were rather spoiled, if I may say so. Am I right so far?'

'Yes, Ābā, you are right.'

'You went to college, got a degree and almost before your result was declared, you got a job in the Co-operative Bank. You were blessed with good looks as well as health and, what is more, you married a girl of your own choice.'

'Yes, that was my Karma.'

'No, Keshar, it was your good fortune, but you did not know it.'

'I thought I was lucky, but when our daughter was born, my wife had no time for me.'

'So, instead of showing her affection, you started to drink. Most of your salary was spent on cheap liquor, which certainly did not help. Your wife had no money of her own, but fortunately you and your brother lived in your family house, so at least she had a roof over her head. I know how she suffered trying to find food and clothing for you three on the 100 rupees you gave her every month.'

'That was her Karma,' said Keshar.

'No, Keshar, that is wrong! How can I explain to you? Karma is really what we make of it. God does not determine our lives; it is up to us to use our God-given talents to improve our lives and to help others. All your actions determine your present and your future. Your Karma in your previous life must have been good, which brought you good fortune in this life. Where is your wife?'

'She went to live with her parents four months ago, and took our daughter with her.'

'Where do you have your meals? You still have your job, haven't you?' asked Ābā.

'I lost my job at the bank because I could not do the work.'

'Why was that?'

'I was drinking even in the mornings.'

'Where do you have your food?'

'Someone gives me a meal sometimes. Sometimes I go to my brother and he gives me ten rupees.'

'Who do you think is responsible for your present condition? Is it your Karma?'

'It must have been written in my fate,' said Keshar, still refusing to accept responsibility for his condition.

'No, Keshar,' said Ābā. 'You did not use your intelligence or education correctly, that is why your wife went away and you lost your job. You must give up drinking that country liquor and try to start again.'

'I have lost my confidence and that is why I drink,' said Keshar.

Keshar's remark made Ābā feel that there was still hope. Ābā still had some prasād left in his bag. He quietly brought it out. 'Here, Keshar, I went to Pandharpūr and brought some prasād from there. Take this and may Vithobā give you courage.'

Keshar took the roasted chickpeas and boiled sweets with reverence and ate them. 'Can you give me ten rupees, Ābā?'

'I am sorry, I can't. Why don't you have a cup of tea and perhaps stop for a meal?' As Keshar nodded his acceptance, Ābā asked Rādhā to make some tea and informed her that Keshar would be staying to lunch.

After lunch Keshar joined his palms in front of him and, bowing his head, uttered the words, 'Namaskār, Ābā.'

Ābā wished him good luck and silently prayed that Keshar would regain his confidence gradually and that their talk would show him the positive aspect of Karma.

And so it was that the month that had brought the unexpected adventure of pilgrimage into Ābā's life ended on a hopeful note—with Keshar's visit.

5

Serpent Worship, Krishna's Birth, Bhakti, Moksha

At the beginning of *Shrāvan*, the fifth month of the Hindu year, Ājī had already spent 20 days in her observance of silent prayer, Yamū and Rādhā had not eaten any rice but were quite happy with unleavened *jowar* bread and vegetables; and the girls had so far done their studies regularly so it appeared that they would be able to keep up the momentum. Ramesh was busy learning the *Bhagavadgitā* off by heart which pleased Ābā immensely.

On the fifth day of *Shrāvan* the Wāiker family rose earlier than usual and after their morning tea and baths were ready to offer pūjā to the Nāga deities. When Yamū and Rādhā brought out the brass tray with the pūjā equipment and placed it on a small stool in the front room, Tārā and Leenā asked their uncle Govind why the pūjā tray was put there instead of in the small family shrine off the middle room.

'We are going to offer worship to a cobra,' said Govind. Gitā, Ramesh and Ābā joined them.

'But, Uncle, a cobra is not God,' said Tārā.

'Why do you think a cobra is not God?'

'Because it does not look like the Rāma image in the temple. I don't remember ever seeing a cobra image in any temple,' said Tārā.

'But you must remember!' said Ramesh. 'You have seen a cobra image in the Shiva temple, around Shiva's neck.'

Then Govind spoke. 'In our *Purānas* we read that every creature in this universe is a part of the Supreme God—Brahman. That is why we offer some cooked rice to birds every day before our lunch. On the *Nāg-Panchami* day we offer worship to Nāga to make sure that the serpents will continue to help us by reducing the number of field mice, and also that they will not do us any harm with their deadly poison.'

When Govind stopped, Ābā took up the explanation.

'In the *Purānas* we also read that Nāgas were not serpents themselves but beings with both human and serpentine qualities; they were superhuman in some respects and helpful to man. The Nāgas are believed to live deep down below the earth's surface. As Ramesh pointed out, the Great God, Shiva, wears a serpent around his throat, and Lord Vishnu sleeps on a large Nāga called *Shesha* during his four month rest. Because a serpent is associated with Shiva as well as Vishnu, most Hindus will offer worship to a living cobra.'

'But a living cobra is dangerous,' said Leenā.

'That's true, but a snake-charmer removes its fangs and makes it harmless,' said Ābā.

'If we cannot offer milk and pop-corn to a living cobra,' said Yamū, coming in from the middle room, 'we can draw snake-figures on a board or we can pin this printed picture to the wall and offer worship.'

Yamū held a printed picture showing nine serpents, representing the nine prominent Nāga deities. As Yamū was pinning the picture to the wall in one corner of the room, the reed flute of a snake-charmer was heard in the street. Govind and Ramesh went to the front door and called the snake-charmer into the front courtyard. As the man placed his flat, round basket on the ground and took out his reed flute, all the members of the family stood around the basket at a safe distance. Yamū and Rādhā held the pūjā tray and Govind lit the ghee lamp and a joss-stick.

The snake-charmer began to play his reed flute, and as he opened the basket a yellow cobra was seen, its body glistening, its eyes bright and its forked tongue flicking from its mouth. All four children were spellbound, as Yamū and Rādhā quickly threw some pop-corn into the basket. They then placed a small bowl of milk near the snake and, moving back, offered the light and incense with a circular movement of the tray in a vertical plane. The snake-charmer pulled the milk bowl near to the basket and to everyone's astonishment, the cobra wriggled its head and dipped its tongue into the milk. The man now used a small cane stick, slightly curved at one end, to place the cobra in the basket, and he played the flute while moving the instrument round and round in front of him. This movement of the flute caught the cobra's attention; it hissed and gradually stretched its neck upwards, about a foot high, and spread its hood, gently swaying to and fro as the flute moved and a steady musical note, similar to the sound of bagpipes, issued from the instrument. As the cobra swayed its hood, Govind uttered a prayer: 'May the Nāgas be pleased with our worship and dispel any fear of snake-bite from this house.'

Gopāl then gave five rupees to the snake-charmer who closed the basket and left the house, looking for another patron. Ājī distributed the pop-corn as prasād to everyone. This was followed by the mid-day meal; Yamū and Rādhā had prepared a special sweet dish of steamed dumplings made from wholemeal flour with chickpea and raw sugar stuffing.

That afternoon, Yamū and Rādhā took the three girls to the Shiva temple on the other side of the river where many children were playing on the rope swings attached to a large banyan tree nearby. Gitā, Tārā and Leenā joined the other girls and played on the swings, returning home before dark in a happy mood.

Nāga-Panchami illustrates the all-inclusive nature of the vibrant and living Hindu faith in which all sorts of beliefs, rituals and practices are tolerated. However, after the exciting experience of the day of serpent worship, life soon settled into a normal secular pattern and was not stirred by any religious or social event until the middle of *Shrāvan*.

Then, two days before the Full Moon day, a letter arrived from Delhi; it was from Latā, addressed to Govind and Gopāl.

Delhi,

Dear Govind-dada,
Thank you for making the donation on our behalf and for sending the coconut as prasād of the Narasimha festival. We gave some of that prasād to our Hindu neighbours who were pleased to receive it.

I hope you get this letter before *Rakshā-Bandhan* day, as I am enclosing two silk threads with yellow baubles, for you and Gopāl-dada.

We are still not sure when we can come to visit you; perhaps after the *Diwali* festival if we manage to get some leave. Our namaskārs to Ābā, Ājī, Yamū and Rādhā. With love to Ramesh, Gitā, Tārā and Leenā.

> Your affectionate sister,
> Latā

Rakshā-Bandhan is a festive occasion with an emphasis more social than religious. The term is derived from two Sanskrit words which mean 'binding a protective thread'. The thread itself is not used as an amulet to ward off evil, but as a token of friendship. In the last century, poor Brahmins used to visit their more affluent relations and acquaintances and, after tying silk threads (or *Rākhis*) to their wrists, would expect money gifts and an assurance of continued patronage. There was a time when this festive occasion was considered to be for the Brahmin Varna only, but in modern India most Hindus exchange a Rākhi to renew ties of friendship.

On the Full Moon day of *Shrāvan*, after their morning baths, Gitā, Tārā and Leenā each tied a silk thread with a yellow bauble to Ramesh's wrist. Then Gitā, acting on behalf of her aunt in Delhi, tied a Rākhi around the wrists of Gopāl and Govind, the same Rākhis that had arrived from Delhi two days previously. Yamū and Rādhā gave Rākhis to their husbands and, finally, Ājī tied a red silk thread to Ābā's wrist.

To everyone's surprise, Rāmji, the carpenter, came to Ābā's house and he and Ābā exchanged Rākhis. After Rāmji left, Gitā spoke. 'Ābā,' she asked, 'why is this day called *Nārali-Paurnimā*?'

'Well, in fact this day is known by three names. In North India it is called *Solono*, but in Gujarat and Mahārāshtra it is called *Rākhi-Paurnimā* or *Nārali-Paurnimā*. People in seaside towns offer a *nāral* (coconut) to Varuna, the Lord of the Waters. Also most people use freshly grated coconut-copra to prepare a special sweet dish today.'

'Last year,' said Gitā, 'I remember Ājī prepared sweet coconut-rice on this day, but I think we are going to have something different this year.'

Ājī had suggested that the special sweet for the day should not be the traditional sweet coconut-rice, because of Yamū's and

Rādhā's avoidance of rice during the *chaturmās*; the suggestion was fully supported by the two daughters-in-law and they had prepared half-moon puris stuffed with fresh coconut and raw sugar.

That very afternoon eight Brahmin neighbours called on Ābā and Govind to finalise the details of the annual non-stop recitation of the *Bhagavadgitā* for eight days and nights from the day after the Full Moon day up to the midnight hour of the eighth day in the dark fortnight of *Shrāvan*. Both Ābā and Govind agreed to take part, so that eight men could read the *Gitā* verses in a 24 hour period, each taking three hours to complete the recitation. A corner in the Krishna temple hall had been chosen, where a wooden seat and a low lectern had been arranged. An oil lamp was provided so that a constant flame would enhance the sanctity of the recitation, and two electric lamps had been arranged to provide sufficient light for the readers. There were two reserve readers who would take over in case of illness. All the readers had to sleep in the temple during the recitation and each had to observe a complete fast for six hours before his reading period.

The *Gitā* recitation began the next day and since Govind and Ābā were involved in a special religious observance, Gopāl was asked by Ābā to supervise all secular affairs of the family for the following nine days. The rota was drawn up in such a way that each reader would be needed at a different three hour session each day; this helped those men who had a job during office hours. Every evening Ramesh also spent some time in the Krishna temple and read the *Bhagavadgitā*, although not as a participant in the week-long recitation.

The eighth day was to be the climax of this special observance and recitation, for at midnight many people from all sections of the Hindu community would gather in the temple to commemorate Lord Krishna's birth. The previous day, when Ābā came home after his *Gitā*-reading session, Ramesh wanted to know where the different mythological stories were recorded.

'Your question is simple enough,' began Ābā, 'but the answer is not so simple to find. Most of these stories are written in our *Purānas*; they were handed down from generation to generation by word of mouth before they were written down. Over the centuries they were repeatedly re-told, some parts of the original were left out and new details were added.

'It is quite possible, of course, that in some cases the written version is in fact the original story; on the other hand, the written version may in fact be an entirely new story. The same story is found in different *Purānas*, written at different times and varying in detailed description.'

'Which is the correct story then?' asked Ramesh.

'Who knows! We can only say that a particular story is found in a particular *Purāna*. The matter is further complicated by the fact that the writers of the *Purānas* do not refer to any historical events in the texts, and that makes it difficult to say exactly when that *Purāna* was written. That means we cannot say which version of the story is the earlier one. For example, the story of Krishna's birth is found in the *Bhāgavata Purāna*, *Harivamsha* and *Brahma Vaivarta Purāna*, and although the main thread is similar, the details vary in each version. These same stories were re-told and recorded in Tamil in South India and, therefore, are a closed book to us who speak Marāthī with a little Hindi and English.'

'But Ābā,' continued Ramesh, 'can we not say when these various sacred books were written down?'

'For centuries, everything was composed and preserved by learning it off by heart. The art of writing came much later. These stories were composed and re-told many times during a period of 3000 years, from the twelfth century before the Christian era to the AD sixteenth century. Many well-known scholars, after a long and deep study of these ancient writings in Sanskrit, have been able to say, only in broad terms, when these books were composed and written down. Most scholars estimate that the *Rig Veda* was composed before 1200 BC and the *Mahābhārata* between 300 BC and AD 300. The *Rāmāyana* comes a little later between 200 BC and AD 200.'

'When were the *Purānas* written down, Ābā?'

'Their dates can be given only approximately. I don't remember all the *Purānas*, but only the important ones: *Bhāgavata* AD 950, *Brahma Vaivarta* AD 750–1550, *Harivamsha* AD 300–500, *Padma Purāna* AD 750 and *Vishnu Purāna* about AD 450.'

'Why did the writers of the *Purānas* ignore the important events that were taking place at the time when they were recording these stories?' asked Ramesh.

'Because, generally speaking, Indians, particularly the ancient

Hindus, had very little historical sense. A lot of our ancient history is reconstructed from the factual accounts of Greek, Persian, Italian and Chinese travellers. There were, of course, exceptions to the general trend, but these records were destroyed by battles, fires, floods and white ants. It is really a wonder that so much has survived in spite of natural and man-made disasters, and that is why Hindus must do their level best to preserve these ancient surviving traditions.'

Their conversation came to an end when Āji and Yamū asked everyone to go into the kitchen/dining room for the evening meal.

The following day Ābā and Govind observed a complete fast all day and at ten o'clock at night the whole family went to the Krishna temple where Bāl-Shāstri, a learned priest, was to read the story of Krishna's birth from the *Harivamsha*.

While the final session of the *Gitā* recitation continued in one corner of the assembly hall of the temple, many people gathered and sat on the floor facing Bāl-Shāstri who sat behind a low lectern, not far from the reader. At half past eleven, the priest began to narrate the story of Krishna's birth, reading a portion of the Sanskrit text and giving his own commentary to explain the text to the silent and attentive congregation.

'In the country of the Shūrasenas, in the fair city of Mathurā, there ruled an ambitious and cruel king named Kamsa. He had deposed his elderly father Ugrasen and become king, soon establishing his harsh and oppressive rule over his subjects. Kamsa had a sister, or, as another version of the story states, a cousin, called Devakī, who was married to Vasudeva, a prince of royal blood from a neighbouring kingdom. As soon as the marriage ceremony was over, Kamsa heard a prophecy whispered in his ear by a supernatural voice, that Devakī's eighth child would kill him. He became alarmed and decided to kill Devakī instantly, but Vasudeva promised to hand over all Devakī's children to Kamsa and thus Devakī was saved. Kamsa, however, not wishing to take any chances, put Devakī and Vasudeva under house arrest, closely guarded by his men, to prevent their escape. Years went by while the couple stayed in their comfortable prison and Devakī gave birth to six children who were killed by Kamsa. When Devakī was with child for the seventh time, the embryo was transferred by a miracle from Devakī to Vasudeva's other wife, Rohini, who gave birth to Balarāma. This miracle was performed by the gods to save Krishna's elder brother. Kamsa was informed that Devakī had had a miscarriage. When Rohini's child was born, it was sent to Nanda, a minor chieftain of the cowherds of Gokul, and Yashodā, his wife.

'Lord Vishnu had become anxious about the people who were oppressed by Kamsa and wanted to destroy him. Long ago Vishnu had killed a powerful demon named Kālanemī, who had become incarnate as Kamsa. When Vishnu heard what Kamsa planned to do with Devakī's eighth child, he decided to manifest himself in a new *Avatār* by entering Devakī's womb and being born as a human baby. Vishnu also employed the goddess Yogamāyā to be born as a girl to Yashodā at exactly the same time as Devakī would give birth to Krishna, Vishnu's *Avatār*.

'In due course of time Devakī and Yashodā became pregnant. Krishna was born on the eighth day of the dark half of *Shrāvan* at midnight. It rained heavily, so that the streets were awash. Lord Vishnu had caused the guards to fall into a deep sleep. As soon as the boy was born, he made himself manifest as Vishnu and asked Vasudeva to carry him across the river Yamunā to Nanda's house, where he would find a little girl born to Yashodā. "Fear not," he said to Vasudeva, "carry me in a basket. No one will see you. The river will divide to let you cross. Place me near Yashodā and bring back the girl. When you have done this, the guards will come out of their deep sleep and inform Kamsa. The rest of what will happen you shall witness with your own eyes." Vishnu then became a dark-skinned and well-formed baby once more.

'Vasudeva carried out Vishnu's instructions to the letter. No one saw him during the entire journey to Nanda's house in Gokul and back. The River Yamunā divided during both crossings. Vasudeva exchanged the babies and, as soon as he placed the little girl near Devakī, the guards stirred from their sleep and the baby girl began to cry loudly. The sound awakened the guards, who promptly told the king that Devakī's eighth child was born.

'Kamsa immediately ran to Devakī's room and saw a bright little girl lying near to Devakī. He picked up the girl by one leg, pushed Vasudeva aside and was about to kill the infant when it escaped from his hand and flew up towards the high ceiling, saying: "Why kill me, O cruel Demon? Your enemy, an incarnation of

Lord Vishnu, lives across the River Yamunā and in due course of time will surely kill you."

'There was a flash of lightning and Yogamāyā disappeared. Thus it was that Lord Vishnu defeated Kamsa's immediate plans, leaving him disappointed, angry and afraid.'

When Bāl-Shāstri finished the story, all the people rose and the ārti was performed, at the end of which milksweets were distributed as prasād. In the early hours, the family returned from the temple.

Towards the end of the month, Ramesh had made good progress in learning the *Gita*. One Sunday morning, after he had read two chapters, he interrupted Ābā in his morning ritual of reading a Marāthī newspaper.

'Ābā, what exactly is meant by *Moksha*?'

'Well, we Hindus believe that our *Ātman*—soul—goes through a series of lives without being destroyed. It is born again and again in new bodies and this long cycle of birth, death and birth again is called *Samsāra*. When an individual Ātman has gathered religious merit—*Punya*—by performing good *Karma*, it is released from the Samsāra. This final release from the cycle of birth and death is called Moksha.'

'How does one's Karma affect Moksha?' asked Ramesh.

'Everything that a person does has an effect which may be good or bad for that person as well as other people. Simply stated, good actions result in *Punya*—merit—and bad actions in *Pāpa*—demerit. So performing right actions increases one's merit, and when all demerit is cancelled, Moksha is achieved.

'The *Bhagavadgita* tells us that Ātman never dies; it abandons a worn-out body and is rehoused in another body. Its body in this life depends on its Karma in a previous existence, and when Ātman exists in certain bodies it gathers more demerit even though it is performing actions according to its *Dharma*—code of moral duty—for that existence. Many thousands of lives are needed for Ātman to attain Moksha.'

'There are four different paths mentioned in the *Bhagavadgita* which lead to Moksha,' Ramesh persisted. 'Which is the best path?'

'You are right, Ramesh. The four paths which the *Gita* mentions are Knowledge, Meditation, Action and Devotion. The path of Knowledge is difficult because one needs a learned *Guru*—teacher—to understand the relationship of Ātman and Brahman. The path of Meditation is also difficult for most people, because everyone has responsibilities which must not be neglected. If one undertakes meditation to concentrate one's mind on the Supreme Spirit, Brahman, by neglecting one's duties, then that meditation will result in demerit. For ordinary individuals the path of Action is very easy to follow, simply by performing one's Dharma—moral duty—according to one's class, stage of life, family traditions and occupation. Doing one's duty without evil intentions is the simplest way to worship God.'

'What about the path of *Bhakti*, Ābā?'

'The followers of this path choose a particular deity such as Krishna or Vithobā and they worship an image of it, do silent prayer, repeating its name, go on a pilgrimage, and dedicate every action to that deity. They must not neglect their Dharma however, otherwise their devotion will not create any religious merit for them.'

'The path of Action seems the easiest,' said Ramesh.

'Yes, at your age, your duty as a student is more important than anything else. This is the time to learn. Perhaps you can learn how to do the 16 stage pūjā of Ganesha next month. I'll speak to Govind about it. You do the pūjā and Govind will recite the Sanskrit mantras.'

'Yes, Ābā,' said Ramesh.

6

Ganesha Festival, Hindu Pūjā, Aims of Life

On the first day of *Bhādrap'd*, the sixth month of the Hindu year, Yamū and Rādhā removed various books, old newspapers and the family photographs from the large alcove in the front room and swept it clean. Then Gopāl painted it and the surrounding area using yellow emulsion paint. The alcove was $1\frac{1}{2}$ foot wide, $1\frac{1}{2}$ foot deep and $2\frac{1}{2}$ foot high with a semi-circular arch at the top. Ramesh and Gitā were helping Govind to stick cut-out flower patterns of brightly coloured paper into the small square panels of a rectangular wooden frame. This decorated frame was to be fixed on two pegs in the wall on either side of the alcove so that visitors would be able to see inside the alcove through the opening in the frame.

The next day Ābā and Govind went to the house of a local sculptor, who earned his living by making clay images of various Hindu deities needed for religious occasions. There he paid 15 rupees, and collected an image of the God Ganesha which they had ordered two months in advance.

They brought the image home and placed it in a copper dish on a small stool in the alcove. When the decorated frame was fixed in front of the alcove and the electric light inside was switched on, the Ganesha image could be seen clearly, even across the front courtyard. The Wāiker family was now ready to celebrate the annual *Ganesha* festival, which is a particularly popular celebration in Western India.

Ganesha is an important minor deity of Hinduism; he is the son of Pārvati and Shiva and ultimately an aspect of the Supreme Spirit, Brahman. Ganesha is the remover of obstacles from man's undertakings, and, as such, he is invoked at the beginning of a

Ganesha, a minor but important Hindu deity

Photograph: *Ann & Bury Peerless*

pūjā, or a ritual for the sacred thread and marriage sacraments, at the commencement of any important undertaking, or at the start of a journey.

In Western India the Ganesha festival is celebrated for ten days, and, in addition to the daily private and public worship of the deity, the social and educational aspect includes plays, musical recitals, public speaking competitions, folk songs and dances.

In order to understand and experience God, Hindu wise men of the past devised *upāsanā*, which is a combination of prayers, pūjā and meditation. To succeed in meditation, some symbol is needed to concentrate one's mind on the infinite *Brahman*, and this is the reason why Hindus have created images of God out of their imagination. *Brahman*, the Supreme Spirit, is formless and is referred to as 'it'. This Supreme Spirit—God—can appear to Hindus in any form they like to worship. Different images represent the various aspects of the Supreme Spirit. If God is to be found in every creature, then 'it' can be represented in many forms. *The images are an aid to worship and not the objects of worship*. Hindus worship only one God through different forms, male and female, human or animal, or half animal, half human.

Ganesha has a human body and an elephant's head. He has four arms and a large belly. In one hand he holds either a rosary or a *pāsha* (snare) symbolising his control over death. In the other hand, he holds a goad and an axe as a combined weapon; the goad to regulate our behaviour and the axe to destroy our ignorance. The other right hand gives a blessing to the devotee and the other left hand offers a sweetmeat as a reward for those whose ignorance has been destroyed. In some images a serpent is coiled around Ganesha's throat, which shows his control over death. His *vāhana* (vehicle) is a mouse or rat, which indicates the deity's concern for all creatures, great or small. From Ganesha's mouth comes the sound '*AUM*', the sacred syllable representing God who is at the heart of life itself.

Ābā felt that since his grandson, Ramesh, had undergone the sacred thread rite, he was qualified to perform the annual Ganesha pūjā. On the fourth day of *Bhādrap'd*, all members of the Wāiker family got up earlier than usual and had their morning bath before seven o'clock. Govind had to conduct many pūjās in the houses of his patrons later on, so he had decided to conduct their own pūjā first. Ājī, Yamū and Rādhā had arranged all the materials on two large brass trays. A small basket held flowers and a variety of leaves especially needed for Ganesha worship. The pūjā utensils were made of copper and three wooden boards were placed on the floor in the front room below the decorated alcove; one for Govind, one for Ramesh and one for the Ganesha image.

As Ramesh took up his seat facing the deity's image, he had before him a copper dish, a copper cup and long spoon, a copper vessel containing fresh, cold water, and another copper vessel with a narrow neck filled with water, on which was placed a coconut. There was a conch shell and a small silver hand-bell. Some fruit, dried copra and raw sugar were placed on a small silver dish. Ābā and the three girls sat nearby on a rough cotton carpet on the floor and closely observed the pūjā.

Ramesh sipped cold water three times from the copper cup as Govind uttered the names of Vishnu. On the fourth name, water was allowed to trickle from the right hand into the copper dish. This *Āchamana*, which involves spooning water into the right palm and then sipping it, was repeated a second time. Govind then recited 20 more names of Vishnu, after which Ramesh was asked to join palms before him and revere Ganesha, personal deities, family deities, deities of the town, of locality, of the house, parents, Laxmi-Nārāyan, all other gods, and any learned persons present, and pray that the pūjā would be completed without any disturbance.

Govind then recited short verses in Sanskrit praising Ganesha, the Goddess Pārvati, the Sun, Brahmā, Vishnu, Shiva and Saraswatī. He then announced the exact location and time of the pūjā in detail:

'Today, in *Brahmā*'s second epoch, under *Vishnu*'s protection, in *Shweta-Vārāha Kalpa*, in the era of *Vivaswān Manu*, in the first quarter of *Kaliyuga*, in India, in the town of Wāi, north of the River *Krishna* and south of the River *Godāvarī*, in *Shalivāhana* era, in the *Varshā* season, on the fourth day of *Bhādrap'd*, I perform pūjā'.

After this, Ramesh was asked to repeat every word. 'I offer worship to Lord Ganesha, according to our family tradition, with my limited knowledge and with whatever is available, in order to gain for myself and our family the blessings described in the *Purānas* and to fulfil the dreams and desires of all my relations assembled here, to ward off all evil from our lives and to secure well-being, stability, long life and prosperity for all.'

Ramesh poured a spoonful of water on his right palm and allowed it to trickle down into the copper dish. Then he announced that he would offer worship to the vessel of water representing the holy rivers of India, the conch shell and the bell.

Govind chanted the *mantra* in Sanskrit: 'This copper vessel is filled with water that represents the purifying waters of the holy rivers Gangā, Yamunā, Godāvarī, Saraswatī, Narmadā, Sindhu and Kāverī. I revere the river goddesses and offer worship.'

As the *mantra* was completed, Ramesh applied sandalwood paste, red kum-kum and turmeric to the side of the vessel, sprinkled a few grains of rice over it and put two flowers above the coconut on the vessel.

The next *mantra* described the holy conch shell. 'At the front of this shell is the Moon, in its belly Varuna, on its back Prajāpati and at the tip holy Gangā and Saraswatī, the goddess of learning. This shell came out of the ocean and Vishnu holds it in his hand. It is revered by the Gods; I also bow to you, O Pānchajanya.' Ramesh offered worship to the conch shell in the same way as he had to the water vessel.

The next *mantra* stressed the importance of the bell. 'The tinkling of this bell summons the Gods and dispels the presence of evil spirits. For that reason I ring this bell and offer worship to it.' Ramesh rang the bell and offered sandalwood paste, kum-kum, turmeric, rice grains and a flower in worship.

Ramesh then joined palms and, closing his eyes, repeated the *Dhyāna mantra* (meditation prayer) as Govind recited the verse at a slower pace.

'I bow to Vishnu, the Lord of the Universe, the dispeller of fear from the living, the object of meditation of the Yogins, the lotus-eyed husband of Laxmi, the supporter of the world, infinite as the sky, having a heavenly body the colour of the clouds, the Lord of the Gods, possessing a serene form and reclining on the coils of Shesha Serpent.'

When the preliminary rituals were completed, Govind directed Ramesh to perform the main pūjā of Ganesha consisting of the following 16 stages:

1 *Āvāhana*: The deity was invoked by sprinkling a few rice grains on the image. A blade of grass dipped in ghee was held near the image, touching its eyes and heart to animate it before the *Prāna-pratisthāpan* (consecration) pūjā could begin.

2 *Āsana*: A few more rice grains were placed below the image in the copper dish to offer the deity a firm seat. When the image was placed in the alcove after this *Prāna-pratisthāpan* (consecration) pūjā, it was not moved until the end of the festival; the daily pūjā was offered to the image while it was in the alcove.

3 *Pādya*: The feet of the image were symbolically washed by touching them with a wet flower.

4 *Arghya*: The deity was offered fresh water as an oblation of reverence. A spoonful of water was poured onto the right palm and allowed to trickle into the copper dish before the worshipper. After Ramesh had offered an oblation of water to the deity, he wiped his hands on a small towel.

A small quantity of a mixture of milk, yoghurt, ghee, honey and sugar was poured into a small dish and placed before the image as a welcoming drink. A drop of it was applied to the mouth of the image.

5 *Āchamanīya*: Once more fresh water was offered to the deity, but this time as a drink; a drop being placed on the hand of the image.

6 *Snāna*: It was assumed that the deity wished to have a refreshing bath. A flower dipped in the yoghurt-honey mixture was used to sprinkle the image lightly, followed by fresh water sprinkling. Warm water, with various body lotions such as saffron and sandalwood paste, was also used for the bath.

7 *Vastra*: A strip of red cloth was draped around the neck and shoulders of the deity, and some cotton wool, tinged with kumkum, was placed around the base of the image. These garments were for warmth.

8 *Yajnopavīta*: The sacred thread, suitably folded into a small loop, was draped around the image so that it rested on the left shoulder and lay across the chest to hang below the right hand.

Govind then asked Ramesh to lift the image along with the copper dish and place it firmly on the little stool in the alcove. When the image was placed in the correct position, the pūjā continued, but now Ramesh had to stand to make the various offerings.

9 *Gandha*: Using the third finger of the right hand, a dab of sandalwood paste was applied to the deity's forehead. Kum-kum, turmeric, vermilion and camphorated charcoal were similarly applied.

10 *Pushpa-patra*: For this consecration pūjā, Ramesh offered the deity red flowers, 21 blades of grass and 20 leaves of different flowering shrubs. Gitā had prepared a small garland of red flowers which Ramesh placed around the neck of the image and arranged other flowers around it as decoration.

11 *Dhoopa*: Two joss-sticks scented with jasmine essence were lit and stuck in a metal holder. These were moved in a vertical circle before the deity and placed in the alcove to the left of the image. Within a few minutes a thread of smoke rose up and its fragrance pervaded the room.

12 *Deepa*: A small ghee-lamp with a single upright wick was lit and similarly offered to the deity to ward off evil spirits. The lamp was then placed in the alcove to the right of the image.

13 *Naivedya*: Now Ramesh placed a dish containing copra and raw sugar before the image in the alcove and, sprinkling it with a few drops of cold water, offered it to the deity as an especially favourite food of Ganesha. Before the mid-day meal, the main sweet dish for the day was also to be offered to the deity. Govind said the appropriate *mantras*, praying that the deity would accept this food offering. Water was offered to wash the hands and as a drink after this meal.

14 *Phala-Tāmboola and Dakshinā*: Fresh fruit (bananas), coconut, betel leaves and betel nuts were offered as an after dinner snack and as a digestive aid. Five rupee coins were placed before the image as a small cash gift (*Dakshinā*).

15 *Pradakshinā*: Where possible, the worshipper is expected to circumambulate the deity. As the image was in the alcove, Ramesh did a complete turn about himself through 360 degrees in a clockwise direction and, joining his palms before him, bowed low and asked the deity to accept the whole pūjā which was offered with devotion and sincerity, and begged forgiveness for any omissions.

16 *Ārti and Mantra-pushpa*: Another ghee-lamp was lit and placed in a metal tray and three small tablets of camphor were also lit in the tray. Songs of praise for Ganesha, Shiva, Devi and

Vishnu were sung by the whole family to the accompaniment of small brass cymbals. At the end of *ārti*, everyone offered flowers to the deity and bowed low in deep reverence. Govind said the benediction verses:

'I prostrate before you and touch your feet. I view your form with adoring eyes. I embrace you with love and offer worship with gladness. I offer light with devotion and humility, O Lord.'

'You are my mother and father, my brother and friend.

'You are my knowledge and my strength. You are indeed my entire existence, O Lord.

'Whatever actions I perform with my body, speech, mind and other sense-organs, whatever I do knowingly or indeed as a habit, I offer it all, without any reservation, to Nārāyana.'

Govind gave everyone a piece of copra and a little raw sugar as *prasād*. Gopāl then fixed the decorated wooden frame on the pegs at either side of the alcove and when the electric light was switched on, the consecrated image of Ganesha could be seen from across the front courtyard.

Ājī, Yamū and Rādhā prepared the special sweetmeat called *Modak*, with rice flour pastry and fresh coconut and raw sugar stuffing. After Govind had conducted pūjās in different houses, he offered the cooked food to Ganesha before the family had their lunch. Ābā, Govind, Gopāl and Ramesh in turn offered the morning and evening worship to Ganesha over the next ten days of the festival.

There were seven public festivals in the seven areas of the town; each had a consecrated image of Ganesha installed in a specially constructed *mandap*—a temporary pavilion—made from bamboo poles with a cloth ceiling. Many people assembled every night at these neighbourhood festivals to listen to folk songs sung by various groups of schoolchildren. The two high schools in the town had arranged special competitions and in one of these Gitā got the second prize of seven rupees for a public speech of five minutes, in which she outlined how this religious festival was used as a political weapon by B G Tilak in the early decade of this century, when public gatherings for political purposes were banned by the British government in India.

On the *Ananta-day* the festival ended. Many images from private homes as well as from the neighbourhood festivals were taken in different processions through the town to the large *Ghāt*—the paved quadrangle—in front of the main Ganesha temple, where, after the final *ārti* and *prasād*, the images were thrown into the river and the consecrated clay was returned to the great elements.

When Ramesh returned from school the next day, Ābā and Govind were having tea in the front room.

'Ābā, I had an argument with two boys who said that Hindus worship many different Gods and that is why they quarrel with each other,' said Ramesh.

'What did you reply?'

'Well, both statements are true; we worship different Gods and Hindus do not get on with each other. I was not able to say much.'

'Ramesh,' said Ābā, 'there is some truth in what the boys said, but the disagreement comes out of ignorance. Hindus worship only One God under different names.'

'Let me tell you the *Mantra of Unity*,' added Govind, 'then you can answer your friends' charges. You can write it down in the original Sanskrit and I will then translate it for you.'

Ramesh wrote the verses as Govind dictated.

'*Yam Vaidikā mantra drishah purānāhā,
Indram, Yamam, Mātarishwānamāhu.
Vedāntino nirvachaniyamekam
Yam Brahma Shabdena Vinirdishanti.* (1)
*Shaivāyameesham shiva itya Vochan,
Yam Vaishnavā Vishnu riti stuvanti.
Buddhas tathārhat iti Bauddha Jaināhā
Sat-shrī-Akālé ticha sikkha santah.* (2)
*Shastéti Kéchit Katichit Kumārah,
Swameeti Mātéti Pitéti Bhaktyā.
Yam prārthayanté Jagadeeshatāram,
Sa éka éva Prabhuradwiteeyah.*' (3)

'Now, here is the translation,' said Govind: ' "There is only One God, the Lord of the Universe, to whom the vedic sages referred as Indra, Yama and Mātarishwan; the vedānta scholars called him One Brahman; the Shaivas call him Shiva; the Vaishnavas praise him as Vishnu; he is the Buddha of the Buddhists; the Arhat of the Jains; the Sikh saints call him Sat-shri-Akāl. He is known as the

Supreme ruler, Kumāra-Swāmi, Master, Mother or Father by his different devotees." '

After writing the translation, Ramesh read it twice and said, 'Uncle Govind, this means that Ganesha is another name for the One God we worship.'

'Exactly,' said Govind, 'Ganesha is one of the many aspects of the One Supreme Spirit, and only those Hindus who do not understand this *Mantra of Unity* quarrel with others.'

'Tomorrow I shall win the argument,' said Ramesh as he went into the middle room to put away his books and prepare to do his homework.

The second fortnight of *Bhadrap'd* is set aside for ancestor worship and towards the end of the month, Āba and Govind performed the annual *shrāddha* by offering *pinda*—balls of boiled rice—to the deceased ancestors, at which point three generations of Āba's paternal and maternal ancestors were mentioned by name. His cousins and uncle were also remembered. In the afternoon the sacred *pindas* were deposited in the river, thus providing food for fish and other creatures.

A few days later Rāmji, the carpenter, who had persuaded Āba to go on a pilgrimage to Pandharpūr, called to see Āba in the afternoon just as Āba was thinking of a cup of tea after his nap. When Rāmji came, Āba called Ājī and asked her to make some tea for their guest.

'Are you getting enough work, Rāmji?' enquired Āba as Rāmji came across the front courtyard and sat on the edge of the rough cotton carpet in the front room.

'Yes, by the grace of Pānduranga, I have sufficient work to fill my belly,' replied Rāmji, 'and as long as He keeps me in good health, I shall be able to follow my *Dharma*.'

'But, Rāmji, our *Purānas* tell us that along with *Dharma*, we should also pursue *Artha* and *Kāma*. We should all try to earn more money than we need to exist so that we can satisfy all our desires and enjoy a few luxuries as well, to improve the quality of our lives.'

At this point Ājī brought in cups of tea for the two men and quietly went back to the kitchen.

'I have earned enough money to fulfil my two important wishes,' said Rāmji, sipping hot tea. 'I was able to send my son to

High School; he is now employed in a bank as a clerk, and I have also been able to buy a radio to listen to when I work.'

'Have you been to Banāras yet?' asked Āba.

'No, I have no real wish to visit Kāshi as long as I am able to go on my pilgrimage to Pandharpūr twice a year. That will surely bring me Moksha.'

'I have also satisfied my wishes,' replied Āba. 'Both my sons are married and have their own families. One daughter lives in Willāyat—in England—and the other is at Delhi. Like you, I must also gradually prepare for Moksha. I shall look forward to visiting Pandharpūr after *Diwāli*.'

When both had finished their tea, Rāmji went away, leaving Āba to muse over the idea of Moksha. It was also time to begin to plan the celebration of *Navarātri* the following month.

7

Gandhi, Navarātri, Conversion to Hinduism

The month of *Ashwin*, the seventh month of the Hindu calendar, coincides with October, and Hindus are busy during this month celebrating festivals dedicated to Pārvati and Laxmi. In the secular pattern of life, schoolchildren prepare for the half-yearly tests, the schools commemorate Mahatma Gandhi in various ways, and farmers are alert, guarding their standing crops, full of hope for a rich harvest.

All schools in the town had decided to encourage their pupils to write a few lines about Gandhi, and the Walker children had prepared their homework which Gopāl and Ābā were asked to read before the pieces were handed in to the teachers. Ābā read Leenā's contribution first.

> Mohandās Karamchand Gandhi was born on 2 October 1869 at Porbandar in Western India. He was a Hindu belonging to a rich family, since his father was chief minister of an Indian state. At the age of 18 he was sent to London to study Law and after three years study he became a barrister in 1891. He came back to India but soon went to practise Law in South Africa. Gandhi tried to help Indians in that country by fighting unjust laws there. When there was war in South Africa, Gandhi organised ambulances to help wounded soldiers.
>
> When he came back to India in 1915, he joined the Congress party and led the Indian people against the British Officers until India became free. He was murdered in 1948.

Ābā handed Leenā's piece to Gopāl and began to read what Tārā, his 11 year old granddaughter, had written:

> We remember Gandhiji today. He was born on 2 October 1869, his wife was called Kasturbā and they had four sons. He had read the writings of John Ruskin and Tolstoy, who was Russian.

He studied the *Bhagavadgitā* and Yeshu Christa's *New Bible*. When he was in South Africa, he decided not to depend on machines and learned farming, cooking, nursing and teaching. When he came back to India from South Africa in 1915, he founded the *ashram* (secluded residence) at Sābarmatī. When he was working for the Congress Party he visited many villages to talk to the people, but he found that the untouchables were asked to sit on one side at these meetings. He always went and sat amongst them.

He felt ashamed that they were badly treated by high caste Hindus so he always treated them kindly. He gave them a new name, *Harijans*, which means children of God. He wanted the Harijans to have the same rights as others and for this he undertook many fasts until he achieved his goal. He never wore a shirt because he said that he must live like most poor Indians. He wore glasses, a short *dhoti*, open sandals and carried a walking stick. Our teacher said Gandhi was a *sant* [saint] like Rāmdās and that was why he was called a *Mahatma*.

Gitā's writing on Gandhi was centred on his political leadership of the Indian National Congress.

Many people have written about Gandhiji so I shall not give details of his life, but only say something of his *satyāgraha*. He insisted on truth and he was a man of peace. He wanted the British to leave India but he did not want Indians to fight the British with guns. He told the people that the foreign rulers passed many laws which were unjust and oppressed the poor people. In 1919 there was much unrest in the Punjab and after the *Jallianwala Bagh* killings Gandhiji started civil disobedience movements. He was against violence but he later realised that his followers were not disciplined enough to remain calm. Violence broke out and people burned many Indian policemen by setting fire to the police station at Chauri-chaura. Gandhiji was disappointed, and he called off the movement. He was arrested in 1922 and sent to prison for six years, but he was released in 1924.

The most important *satyāgraha* was in 1930 at Dāndī in protest against the salt monopoly of the government. Gandhiji said that salt was necessary for the poor people since they could not afford other spices, and therefore salt laws were unjust. He started with about 80 people from his *ashram* at Sābarmatī, and by the time he reached Dāndī on the coast, his followers had grown into thousands. He broke the salt laws and was sent to prison; his followers were also sent to jail.

Gandhiji was again the leader in the 'Quit-India movement' in 1942. He was sent to prison for about three years. Just before independence, there were riots in Bengal and Bihar. Gandhiji was 77 years old then, but he walked in those areas urging Hindus and Muslims to follow the principle of *Ahimsā*, non-violence.

In 1948, he was shot by a Hindu who did not respect his political ideas. Gandhiji preached and practised *Ahimsā* all his life but he died a violent death.

'Gopāl, our Gitā has done her homework well. Here... you have a look at this,' said Ābā, as he handed over Gitā's exercise book. He then started to read what Ramesh had written:

Mahatma Gandhi will be remembered for using the Hindu principle of *Ahimsā* for gaining independence for India in a century when Europe was trying to solve her political problems by long drawn-out wars which claimed many million lives. *Ahimsā* was the main principle for Gandhi, but his followers often turned his peaceful movements into violent riots.

The second important principle which he followed was insisting on truth, and he never gave up his self-discipline when many about him were losing their heads.

He turned the National Congress into an Indian people's movement and opposed the British Government in India by activating his civil disobedience campaigns. He cheerfully went to prison for the national cause. He tried to remove the caste divisions in Hindu society by example, by insisting that the untouchables were 'children of Hari'.

I think he failed to persuade Hindus and Muslims to live in peace in his lifetime, but, since independence, many Muslims have lived peacefully with their Hindu neighbours although they don't really respect Hinduism which is the religion of the majority of people in India. Gandhiji was also opposed to machines, and if he had been younger and had entered the government of free India in 1947, India would not have been able to start heavy industries like steel plants and electrical machinery. He was a great man and a prominent Hindu of this century.

When Ābā and Gopāl read the homework, they were very pleased to note that the new generation were learning to think for themselves.

As the Hindu calendar is based on the waning and waxing of the Moon, each month is divided into a light and dark fortnight. On the first day of the light half of *Ashwin*, Govind performed the daily *pūjā* of the family deities and was ready to offer special worship to Pārvatī, the Mother Goddess and consort of Shiva. Yamū appeared near the door of the family shrine and placed a newly cleaned copper dish with some rice grains and a basket containing a single-strand garland of fresh marigolds on the floor. Govind then placed the copper dish below a peg in the wall which was strong enough to hold a brass oil-lamp. He then placed a small brass image of the *Devi* (Goddess) on the bed of rice in the copper dish and offered worship. Then he suspended the garland from the peg so that the free end just rested in the copper dish about two feet below. Finally he lit the lamp, which was to be kept burning day and night for nine days. A fresh garland would be added each day, thus, on the last day there would be nine marigold garlands hung from the peg.

This festive occasion is called *Navarātri*—nine nights—and is a time for private worship of the *Devi (Pārvatī* or *Durgā*). At lunch on the first day Gitā and Tārā wanted to know why a special sweet called *Puran-polee*—chapatis stuffed with a mixture of cooked chickpeas and raw sugar—was prepared. Their question was answered by Rādhā, which surprised and pleased Ābā and Ājī.

'Today starts the festival of Navaratri in honour of *Devi-Pārvatī*. We always cook *Puran-polee* on the first and the last days.'

'How long does Navaratri last?' asked Gitā.

'As the word suggests, nine days and nights,' said Rādhā.

'We have a lady teacher from Calcutta who teaches English and she was saying, when I handed in my homework about Gandhiji, that she missed the *Durgā-pūjā* festival, since she lived and worked in Western India. What is *Durgā-pūjā*, auntie?'

'Durgā is another name for Pārvatī. In North India, especially in Bengal, Durgā-pūjā is celebrated as a public festival during Navaratri, very similar to the way we celebrate the Ganesha festival in Mahārāshtra. Why don't you ask your Bengali teacher for details when you see her in school tomorrow?' replied Rādhā.

The public festival of Durgā-pūjā   *Photograph: School of Oriental and African studies*

The very next day Gitā came home from school eager to describe Durgā-pūjā, as her teacher had told her; so, after the evening meal, as Tārā and Leenā sat near Ābā and Ājī in the front room, Gitā told the younger girls about it.

'Durgā-pūjā originated with a sect who worshipped *Shakti* (*Devi*) instead of a male deity. The festival lasts for nine days and nights but the main pūjā, called the *Sandhi-pūjā*, is offered on *Mahā-Ashtamī*, the eighth day. People offer pūjā at a public festival where an image of Durgā is installed. Durgā is represented as a tall woman with a fair complexion. She has eight arms in which she holds different weapons. In one of her lower arms she holds a tuft of hair from a demon whom she has killed. The demon was Mahishāsura, in the form of an angry buffalo. Along with Durgā, smaller images of Saraswatī, Laxmi, Ganesha and Kārtik are also installed.

'Gitā,' asked Tārā, 'do the people in Bengal offer *Puran-polee* to Durgā?'.

'I don't know,' said Gitā, 'but the teacher said that a goat is killed as an offering. They also offer fruit and milk.'

'Do they eat that goat?' asked Leenā.

'Yes,' said Ābā. 'As prasād. Many thousands of years ago our Aryan ancestors used to eat meat when they lived in a cold climate, but gradually most Hindus became vegetarians; today, many Hindus eat meat except on festival days.'

'I am glad we don't eat meat,' said Tārā.

'So am I,' said Ābā. He stood up, and told the girls that they should study a little before retiring for the night.

Although Navarātri is celebrated as a Devi festival in Gujarat, Bengal and Mahārāshtra, in North India, Rāma, the hero of Rāmāyana, is commemorated through the enactments of *Rāma-Leelā*—the exploits of Rāma. For the nine days of Navarātri, different episodes of the Rāma epic are presented as plays with colourful costumes and music. These dramatic representations in the open air are designed to instruct illiterate audiences in the moral teachings of the epic. The incidents associated with the war in Lankā between Rāma's forces led by Hanumān, the monkey chief, and the forces of Rāvana are dramatised. Hanumān is worshipped for his loyalty, personal devotion and sheer physical strength and in almost every village there is a Hanumān temple.

When an incident from the epic is presented on stage, a group of singers recite the appropriate verses from the original poem. The *Rāma-Leelā* ends with the defeat and death of Rāvana, whose effigy is set on fire and blown up with fireworks at the conclusion of the festival on the *Dasserah* day, the tenth day of the month. Some Hindus associate the Rāma story with *Diwāli*, but they are in the minority.

On the Dasserah day, after their early morning baths, Ābā, Govind, Gopāl and Ramesh collected various implements in the house, brought them to the front room and arranged them in one corner—a pick, two shovels, an iron bowl normally used in the garden to carry loose earth, two trowels, three pairs of scissors, three axes, a dagger and an old sword which was usually kept hidden in a cupboard in the middle room. They all took turns at offering worship to each implement, using sandalwood paste, red kumkum powder, turmeric, rice grains and flowers. Rādhā had made a few short garlands of marigolds which Govind attached to some of the implements. A joss-stick was lit and soon its fragrance diffused through the room. As the men finished this pūjā, Gitā, Tārā and Leenā came out to the front room.

'Ābā, why have you offered pūjā to these axes and scissors?' asked Gitā.

'Well, Gitā,' said Ābā, 'today is the festival of *Vijayā-dashami*. Four hundred years ago when there were small kingdoms fighting with each other in India, on the Dasserah day the armies of the Hindu kingdoms used to start preparations for battles, sharpening their swords and lances. This symbolic *pūjā* commemorates an even older event described in the *Mahābhārata*, the War between the Kuru and Pāndava princes. I expect you remember how the Pāndavas lost everything, and had to spend 12 years in the forest and one more year without being recognised. At the end of the thirteenth year, the sons of Pandu came out of their exile, collected their weapons which they had hidden in the hollow of an Ashmantaka tree, and prepared for battle to win their share of the kingdom. It is this event that is remembered in this part of India, while the people in North India will remember Rāma when they celebrate the *Rāma-Leelā* festival.'

'Ābā, what will you do with these tools?' asked Tārā.

'We will not do anything with them, but all four of us will walk to the western boundary of our town where many men will also come, all dressed in their new clothes and wearing colourful turbans.'

'Ābā, may I carry this dagger when we go out this afternoon?' asked Ramesh.

'Yes, Ramesh, but don't pull it out of its case. As I was saying, Gitā,' Ābā continued, 'when we go to the spot outside the town, Govind will offer worship to an Ashmantaka tree and we shall exchange the leaves of that tree with everyone else. The men will be from different castes but they will all be Hindus. It will be a peaceful gathering of men exchanging friendship.'

When the men returned in the evening, Govind had brought with him a twig of the Ashmantaka tree which he hung on a wall-peg in the front room as a token reminder of the moral of the event in the *Mahābhārata*: that is, after all peaceful methods have failed, man must be prepared to take up arms in defence of a just cause.

After the Full-Moon day, Ābā received a letter from his daughter Neelā who lived in Leicester in England, with her architect husband Ganesh and their daughter Sheila.

Leicester, England

My dear Ābā

About three weeks ago we attended a religious ceremony here which is very rare these days and I am sure you and Govind will be interested to read about it.

The son of a Hindu friend of ours fell in love with a British girl who comes from a devout Christian family. The parents of the couple fully approved of their wish to marry and the young lady decided to become a Hindu, before announcing her engagement. Ganesh and I were invited along with 50 others to witness the conversion ritual which took place before the family shrine in the house owned by the boy's parents. The girl, who was called Jean, wore a silk sari with a matching blouse and her fair hair was put up in a bun. Jean's parents, brother and sister were present at the ceremony.

As part of the *welcoming*, Jean was given a coconut at the entrance to the house and as she made her way towards the family shrine in the front room she was showered with flower petals while the officiating Hindu *Pandit* recited mantras. Jean placed the coconut before the Ganesha image and made her namaskār, bowing low before Ganesha. She picked up the coconut, then handed it to and received it back from all members of the boy's family as they welcomed her. When she did namaskār before the boy's parents and elder aunts she was given money in welcome. Milksweets were distributed amongst all present to sweeten the welcome. Then followed the purification ritual.

For the *purification* Jean was required to be freed from the spiritual impurities or taints that attached to her spirit, through body, speech, mind, food eaten or discarded, liquids drunk and not drunk, actions performed knowingly or unwittingly, and by any other means. The Pandit annointed her with ten different substances. They were: *Bhasma* (ash), *Mrittikā* (earth), *Pushpa* (flower), *Phala* (fruit), *Vanaspati* (plant), *Dugdha* (milk), *Dhānya* (grain), *Dhana* (money), *Suvarna* (gold), and *Gangā-Jala* (Ganges water). For the last annointing, Ganges water was lightly sprinkled on Jean by a married woman present, while the Pandit recited eight verses in praise of the holy *Gangā*.

Jean sat before the Pandit and, sipping water three times, announced her intention of giving up her Christian faith to become a Hindu. Then she performed the *Gāyatri Havan* and propitiated the planets after receiving a Hindu name and emblems of Hinduism. Jean held a crucifix in her hands and said the Lord's prayer. She promised to honour Christ as a prophet of all humanity and declared that she was leaving the smaller Christian faith to join the greater Hindu faith of all humanity; she asked for Christ's blessing in her determination to understand her new faith. The Pandit assured her that Hinduism was not opposed to Christianity and she announced that she would always have devotion for Christ and pray for his direction. Jean placed a flower on the cross and offered the symbol of her former faith to the Pandit. She then performed *Āchamana*, sipped water three times and offered prayers; the Pandit applied water to her eyes.

After Jean had renounced her Christian faith, the Pandit explained to her the ten core principles of the Hindu faith which she would have to accept.

1 Recognition of the authority of the Vedas.

2 Belief in the teachings of the *Dharma-shastras*, the *Brahma-Sutras*, the *Upanishads* and the *Bhagavadgitā*.

3 Belief in One Supreme Spirit—*Brahman*.

4 Belief in the transmigration of *Ātman*—life force.

5 Adherence to *Satya*—truth.

6 Practising *Ahimsā*—non-injury.
7 Refraining from stealing.
8 Non-avoidance of physical labour.
9 Accepting the worship of images as symbols of the different aspects of Brahman.
10 Following the *Varna, Jāti, Kula* and *Āshrama Dharma* to the best of her ability.

Jean thought over the words of the Pandit, then took water in her right palm and sipped it, thus signifying her acceptance of the tenets of her new faith. The Pandit recited verses from the *Bhāgavata-puran* and the *Rāmāyana* for her to hear, and then he and his assistant recited the fifteenth chapter of the *Bhagavad-gitā*. Jean held the printed copy of the *Gitā* in her right hand and promised to observe the Hindu *Dharma*. Jean was then given a Hindu name; it was Jayashree, which was whispered into her right ear by a senior lady in the boy's family. Some honey was poured on a wooden platter and a gold ring was rubbed in it. Jayashree was asked to lick the honey, using the third finger of her right hand, to sweeten her personality. She also licked honey from a betel leaf. The Pandit told her that she would be successful in all her undertakings since her new name Jayashree meant victory incarnate. She was given a small piece of *burfee*—a milk-sweet—by each member of the boy's family. She then offered worship to the presiding deity of the family.

She was now a Hindu ready to receive emblems of her new faith. Jayashree was given a pendant of deer-skin on red/yellow cotton thread to wear. The assistant priest held a silver disc with engravings of Ganesha and the AUM symbol in his right hand with some rice, while the Pandit recited verses from the *Rigveda*. This AUM symbol was given to Jayashree for her private worship and meditation. The Pandit chanted *mantras* from the *Taittirīya Āranyaka*—a sacred text—and instructed Jayashree to emulate only the righteous actions of others, to honour her mother, father, Guru, guests and nation, to speak the truth, never to neglect her studies and to be diligent in her religious and family duties. Jayashree accepted this advice by performing the *Āchamana*.

The *Gāyatri Havan*—worship of the sacred fire—was performed to avert evil from Jayashree's life and to obtain for her Agni's blessings.

First, Jayashree sipped water three times and the Pandit chanted praises of Agni, sprinkling water around the sacred fire in a clockwise and anti-clockwise direction. The fire was lit in a metal container using *samidhā*—small sticks of wood. *Dhānya*—grain—oblations were offered to Agni, Prajāpati, Surya (Sun), Chandra (Moon), Mangal (Mars), Budha (Mercury), Guru (Jupiter), Shukra (Venus), Shani (Saturn), Rāhu, Kétu, Rudra (Shiva), Gauri (Pārvati), Ganesha, Saraswatī, Vishnu, Mahālaxmi, deity of speech, and Varuna, to propitiate the planets and other deities.

During the second part of the Havan, 24 ghee oblations were offered to Gāyatri while the Gāyatri Hymn was chanted 24 times. One oblation each was offered to the guardians of the ten directions, beginning with East and continuing in a clockwise direction. They were Indra (East), Agni (South East), Yama (South), Nirrata (South West), Varuna (West), Vāyū (North West), Soma (North), Īshwara (North East), Brahmā (upper atmosphere) and Prithivi (Earth).

In the third part, the *Pūrna-ahuti* (complete oblation) consisting of betel nuts, rice grains and ghee, was offered to all deities and Brahman. The Pandit chanted the peace prayer for all cosmic creation, and a little ash from the sacred fire was dabbed on Jayashree's forehead to obtain for her faith, intellect, success, learning, grasping power, wealth, strength and long life.

There were 16 lamps arranged on a tray, all but one lit, representing the phases of the Moon. The nine planets were represented by nine betel nuts on a bed of rice on another tray and these were offered worship by the boy to ward off evil forces indicated by their positions in the horoscopes of the couple.

Engagement: Jayashree was offered in marriage to the boy and was accepted by the boy's parents who reassured the girl's parents that she would be looked after by the whole family. Three generations of the boy's and girl's ancestors were mentioned by name and coconuts were exchanged by the parents of the couple. The couple also exchanged rings at this engagement. Sugar was distributed to all persons present and there was a feast for all.

Ābā, this was the first time that I have witnessed such a conversion to Hinduism. I hope it interests you as much as it interested me. Ganesh and Sheila are both well. My namaskārs to Ājī, Govind, Yamū, Gopāl and Rādhā. Blessings to the youngsters.

Your affectionate daughter,
Neelā

As the festival of *Diwāli* approached, Ājī, Yamū and Rādhā were busy preparing various delicacies for the occasion. It was decided to paint the front room so Govind, Gopāl and Ramesh were busy with white emulsion and brushes. All was ready two days before the festival was due to begin. That afternoon Vasant came home for *Diwāli* from Bombay as his College was closed for a three week vacation.

On the thirteenth day of the dark fortnight of *Ashwin* the festival of *Diwāli* begins. That evening Yamū, the elder daughter-in-law of Ābā and Ājī, prepared a clay lamp with a horizontal wick and filled it with groundnut oil. As she brought it into the front courtyard, Tārā and Leenā were curious.

'Auntie, why do we have only one lamp?' asked Tārā.

'This evening, we offer a single flame lamp to Yama, the Spirit of Death. Yama rules over the southerly direction so the flame will point to the south when I light the lamp.'

'Do we do anything else this evening?' asked Leenā.

'No, nothing else,' replied Yamū, 'but you two can light some sparklers before dinner.' As the two girls played with sparklers, Ramesh lit a string of firecrackers and the noise filled the whole house. The evening of *Yama-deepa-dāna* was the start of the festival for the Wāiker family.

The following day everyone was up by five o'clock and after their morning tea, the ceremonial bathing began. The men's heads and bodies were rubbed with perfumed oil before they had a bath. Ramesh and Vasant were the first to bathe, followed by Gopāl, Govind and Ābā. The girls and the three women followed, and after they had all bathed and changed into clean clothes, they had breakfast. Yamū and Rādhā served the stuffed pastries, flattened rice savoury mixture and some semolina *lādoos*—balls of sweetened and fried semolina. Govind had offered the daily worship to family deities before breakfast.

This second day of Diwāli is called *Naraka-chaturdashi* and commemorates Vishnu's victory over a powerful demon called *Naraka-Asura*. This legend is found in the *Bhāgavata* which is the main collection of Vishnu legends. The house and its surrounds are illuminated with clay lamps every evening, for the word *deepāwalee* means a row of lamps; thus *Diwāli* is a popular abbreviation of the word *deepāwalee*.

The third day of Diwāli is the last and the darkest day of *Ashwin*, and on this day special worship is offered to the Goddess Laxmi, consort of Vishnu; Laxmi is the goddess of good fortune and wealth. So that evening Ābā placed some coins, rupee notes, gold rings, necklaces and silver drinking cups on a bed of rice in a large silver tray under the Ganesha alcove in the front room. Rādhā and Gitā drew *Rangoli* patterns on the floor, using coloured powders, in which a lotus flower motif was prominent. Ājī brought a copper vessel filled with water and placed a coconut on it with a few mango leaves for decoration. Gopāl placed his cheque book and the household account book on the tray and offered pūjā to Laxmi symbols, while Govind chanted the appropriate *mantras* and directed the worship. All doors were kept open so that Laxmi could enter the house, which was illuminated with small oil lamps. The girls lit sparklers while Vasant and Ramesh set off some more fireworks and firecrackers. *Laxmi pūjan* is mainly a festival for merchants, at the time when the account books are closed; after the pūjā, the new financial year begins.

8

Diwāli, Silent Worship, Vishnu Shrines

The fourth day of *Diwāli* is the first day of the month of *Kārtik* and it is called *Bali-pratipadā*. On that day Gopāl had a chance to instruct his daughters Tārā and Leenā in the mythological significance of the fourth and fifth days of Diwāli. 'Do you know why today is called *Bali-pratipadā?*' he asked Tārā.

'I know it is called *pratipadā* because it is the first day of *Kārtik*, but I don't know anything about the word *Bali*.'

'Well, there is a story in the *Purānas* that there was once a very powerful king named Bali. He prayed very sincerely and God made him even more powerful. Then Bali began to oppress people everywhere. Lord Vishnu decided to control Bali and remove the prevailing misery. Vishnu took on a new Avatār, the form of a small boy; he is known as *Vāman*, or dwarf. Vishnu had heard that Bali was very generous, so he went to Bali's palace and asked to see the king. Bali was in a generous mood. He said to Vāman, "Ask for anything and you shall have it". Vāman said: "I only want enough space to walk three steps". As soon as Bali agreed, Vāman, who was really Vishnu, changed his appearance and became very large. He took one step and occupied the Heavens; with the second step he covered the whole Earth.'

'But there was no more space left for the third step,' said Leenā.

'Yes, you are right, Leenā. So Vishnu said, "Where shall I place my foot for the third step, O king?" The king knelt before Vishnu who placed his foot on Bali's head and pushed him into *Patāla*—the nether world.'

'But how is Bali connected with *Diwāli?*'

'Vishnu was pleased with Bali's generous nature, however, so he declared that people on Earth should remember King Bali by having a feast on this day, and giving presents to friends and relations.'

'Are we going to get presents today?' asked Tārā.

'Only Ājī, Yamū and Rādhā will get presents today, but you two and Gitā will get your presents tomorrow. On this day a married woman gets a present from her husband, but you will get your presents from your brother and cousin on the *Yama-dwitīyā* day, which is tomorrow,' explained Gopāl.

'Tell us why it is called *Yama-dwitīyā*,' Tārā asked him.

'In another legend we read that Yama—the Spirit of Death—visited his sister, Yamunā, on the second day of *Kārtik*. She welcomed him and prepared a feast for him. Yama was very pleased and declared that people on Earth should visit their sisters and honour them with presents.'

'What have Vasant and Ramesh got for us for presents? Do you know?' asked Leenā.

'I don't know, but you will find out tomorrow,' Gopāl told her.

On the Diwāli day, Ājī, Yamū and Rādhā received an expensive sari each from their respective husbands and the family enjoyed *shri-khand*—a sweet dish made from natural yoghurt—with puris for lunch. The evening was made more joyous with illuminations and fireworks. Vasant and Ramesh let off large firecrackers which made a deafening noise.

On sister's day, Gitā, Tārā and Leenā fussed over the two boys, applying perfumed oil to their heads and bodies before their bath. The girls then served Vasant and Ramesh their special breakfast, for which Gitā with her mother's help had prepared a savoury dish of soaked, pressed rice with freshly grated coconut and green coriander. Tārā and Leenā coaxed the boys into eating some half-moon pastry and *lādoos* made from chickpea flour and raw sugar.

'Vasant, I think you and Ramesh should give the girls their presents before lunch.' Āba suggested this slight change in the traditional time of giving presents in the evening, because he felt that the girls should enjoy their presents during the rest of the day.

When the women had prepared lunch, Gitā made preparations for the sister's day ritual. Two wooden boards were placed on the floor near the household shrine and the girls drew *Rangoli* designs round them with a floral motif. The auspicious red kum-kum powder, along with yellow turmeric, was used to embelish the design and to ward off evil spirits. Gitā brought the copper dish from the kitchen. Into it she had placed the ghee lamp, rice grains, a gold ring, betel nut and a flat silver box containing kum-kum and turmeric. Vasant and Ramesh sat on the boards facing east. Gitā applied a dab of kum-kum to their foreheads, and sprinkled a few rice grains on their heads. She then moved the betel nut and the ring in clockwise and anti-clockwise directions around Vasant's head and placed the two articles in his right hand. She picked up the copper dish with the lamp, which was lit by Rādhā, and moved it three times in a vertical circle before Vasant. Placing the dish on the floor, she bent low and offered a namaskar—a salutation. Vasant gave her a sari with a matching blouse piece, ten rupees, the betel nut and ring. Gitā performed the same ritual for Ramesh who gave her ten rupees as a present. When Tārā and Leenā moved the lamp to ward off evil from the lives of Vasant and Ramesh, Rādhā stood behind the girls and held the copper dish to make sure that there was no mishap with the ghee lamp. Vasant gave the younger girls saris, which Yamū and Rādhā had purchased and packed beforehand, and ten rupees each; while Ramesh gave them ten rupees each. The sister's day rituals, the presents, and an exchange of affection brought their Diwāli celebrations to a close.

The Festival of Diwāli is celebrated differently by Hindus in other parts of India, but in spite of the local and regional variations, it is dedicated to Vishnu and his consort Laxmi. Apart from the rituals of *Laxmi-pūjā*, the offering of light to Yama and bathing, this festival is a time to renew bonds of affection and love between husband and wife, between brother and sister; a time for careful budgeting, for rich food, new clothes; a time for enjoyment and good neighbourliness. During Diwāli is also a time for friends and neighbours to visit each others' houses and enjoy the seasonal refreshments. In particular, *Bali-pratipadā* day is considered auspicious for starting new undertakings.

The day after the sister's day ritual, life in the Wāiker household began to follow a more secular pattern again. Ābā was busy in the middle room collecting various items of clothing and folding them neatly to pack into a small cloth bag in preparation for his second pilgrimage to Pandharpūr, marking the end of chaturmās. Vasant read a newspaper, while Ramesh was learning to recite the

Bhagavadgitā from memory. Both boys were thus engaged in the front room when Ābā came out of the middle room and sat on the rough cotton carpet. When Ramesh had stopped his chanting, Ābā spoke.

'How many chapters of the *Gitā* can you remember, Ramesh?'

'I can recite 11 chapters, but not entirely from memory. I need to look at the book from time to time. I am now starting chapter 12, which is about Bhakti.'

'You have done well since you started learning to read the verses in May. I am pleased,' said Ābā.

'Ābā, this twelfth chapter is quite short but very difficult to understand,' said Ramesh.

'When you have completed your college education and are a little older, you may understand some of the more difficult parts of the *Bhagavadgitā*. For the present, try to learn the correct way of saying the Sanskrit verses.'

'Ābā, if God is without any form,' Ramesh wanted to know, 'how is it that we offer the 16 stage pūjā to an image? How do we know that particular image is God?'

'Well, it is all a matter of man's imagination and faith. The wise men who wrote the *Upanishads* tell us that the Supreme Spirit—Brahman—is indeed without any form and is to be found everywhere. Very few people can comprehend the abstract Brahman, that is why ordinary Hindus are given full freedom to imagine Brahman in any shape or form which they can understand.'

'Is Brahman male or female?' asked Ramesh.

'It can be anything we imagine it to be. Different images like Vishnu, Ganesha, Shiva, Pārvatī, Laxmi, Hanumān or Garuda, the divine eagle, represent different aspects of Brahman. Ordinary people need images as symbols to worship God, but learned philosophers are able to understand the abstract idea that is Brahman. Have you heard of Shanker-Āchārya?'

'No. Who was he?'

'He was a great scholar who lived in the eighth century, and in his short life of 32 years he wrote commentaries on the *Vedanta Sutras* of Bādarāyana as well as the *Bhagavadgitā*. When he saw that people around him were doing the 16 stage pūjā, he wrote a poem to emphasise the true, formless and all-pervasive nature of Brahman.'

'Is it very long and very difficult to learn?'

'No. You could learn it off by heart,' said Āba. 'It is called *Mānasa-pūjā*—silent worship—and the great Āchārya points out how it is impossible to perform the 16 stage pūjā of Brahman, because each stage involves personification of a divinity which has no personality or attributes. Such rituals can have no meaning or relevance to an impersonal, formless Godhead. You did the Ganesha pūjā so the stages should be quite familiar to you. Vasant also did the Ganesha pūjā two years ago, so he will also remember the stages,' he added, looking at Vasant.

'Yes, I remember most of the stages, Āba,' said Vasant, now putting down his newspaper and eager to listen to Āba.

'I'll give the name of the stage first and then explain what the *Āchārya says about it*.

'*Āvāhana* (invocation): "Since you fill this entire cosmos and are already here, O Lord; whence can I invoke you?"

'*Āsana* (offering a seat): "You are the supporter of everything; how can I offer you a seat?"

'*Pādya-Arghya* (washing of feet, oblation of welcome): "You are already clean; how can I cleanse you further by offering water for washing your feet; by offering an oblation of welcome?"

'*Āchamana* (sipping water for ritual purity): "You are already pure, O Lord; how can my offering of *Āchamana* increase your ritual purity?"

'*Snāna* (bathing): "You are free from impurities; how can I offer you water for bathing?"

'*Vastra* (clothes): "A multitude of creatures are contained in you, O Lord; how can I offer you sufficient clothing?"

'*Yajnopavita* (sacred thread): "You, O Lord, are in the inter-space which makes it impossible for me to put the sacred thread around your left shoulder!"

'*Pushpa* (flowers): "You are free from desire, O Lord; how can these fragrant flowers bring you enjoyment?"

'*Gandha* (sandalwood paste): "You are without any material body, O Lord; how can I anoint you with sandalwood paste?"

'*Alamkār* (ornament): "You are endowed with divine grace, O Lord; how can earthly ornaments enhance your grace?"

'*Naivedya* (food offering): "You are eternally free from hunger, O Lord; how can I offer you food?"

'*Tāmbūla* (digestive aid): "You never have a meal, O Lord; how can I offer you a digestive aid?"

'*Pradakshinā* (circumambulation): "You are endless, O Lord; how can I circumambulate you?"

'*Namaskār* (obeisance, homage): "If you and I are one, O Lord; how can I offer homage to myself?"

'*Stavan, Neerānjana* (praise, light): "Even the Vedas cannot understand you, who are radiant; how can I, a mere mortal, attempt to praise you and offer you light, O Lord?"

'*Visarjana* (dissolution): "O Lord, you occupy every space in this cosmic creation; where, indeed, can I attempt your dissolution?"

'So you see, Vasant, thus the great *vedānta* scholar explains the *Nirākār* (formless), *Nirguna* (without attributes) and *Sarva-Vyāpī* (all persuasive) nature of Brahman, as stated in the *Upanishads* and points out that man has recourse only to silent worship since the 16 stage earthly pūjā is a philosophical and practical impossibility.'

'But, Ābā,' Ramesh asked, 'does this mean that my Ganesha pūjā was wrong?'

'No, not at all. The *Āchārya was simply explaining the true nature of Brahman. The Bhagavadgitā*, in chapter 12, specifically says that ordinary Hindus should worship Brahman through different images, remembering that the image is only a representation of the eternal Supreme Spirit.'

The following morning Ābā and Rāmji, taking with them a few clothes and some money, left for their pilgrimage to Pandharpūr. The pilgrims had to reach the shrine by the eleventh day of *Kārtik* since the four month period of fasting and special observances comes to an end on that day.

About a week after Ābā had gone on his pilgrimage, Vasant read a report in the newspaper; it concerned the protest march and demonstration by high caste Hindus against reserved jobs and university places for scheduled castes in Gujarat. He passed the paper over to his father, Govind, then to his uncle Gōpal, and then to his cousin, Ramesh. They all read the report.

'Uncle Gopāl, why are different *jātis* in our society unable to get along with each other?' Vasant asked.

'I suppose it's because the upper castes think that they are superior to others. They have advantages which they want to preserve, but the government is trying to give equal opportunities to those sections of the community who have been kept backward for centuries.'

'But surely this help for the scheduled castes deprives the upper castes of jobs and places in colleges of higher education,' Vasant insisted. 'Many clever children from upper castes, in fact, don't get into the college because half the places are reserved for the scheduled castes.'

'The situation will change in time and, for the present, the higher castes will have to direct their talents towards commerce.'

'Uncle Govind,' said Ramesh, 'I'm interested in how the Vedic Aryans organised their society? When did the *jāti* difference begin?'

'The Aryans who entered India about 4000 years ago were trying to find a new place to settle down. They had to conquer the original inhabitants and absorb them into the new society. This society was divided into four *varnas* (categories) by about 1000 BC. The Aryans certainly had the three twice-born *varnas*, probably before they established themselves in their new land. These varnas were classes based on function; the *Brahmins* were teachers and priests, the *Kshtriyas* looked after the administration and protected the community from foreign enemies, and the *Vaishyas* tended cattle, cultivated the land and engaged in trade. By the time the *Upanishads* were composed, the fourth varna—*Shūdras*—was added to the list; these were probably the conquered original inhabitants, who were artisans like basket-weavers, masons and potters. The *Purusha* hymn of the *Rig Veda* explains the origins of the four varnas; the Brahmins were in the mouth, the Kshtriyas in the arms, the Vaishyas in the legs and the Shūdras in the feet of the Cosmic Person. This classification was considered of divine origin and could not be modified for secular reasons; it was based on the nature of people belonging to the same varna and broad outlines of functions of each varna were defined in the *Manu Smriti* and the *Bhagavadgitā*.'

'I remember the verse from the *Bhagavadgitā*,' said Ramesh, eagerly. 'It comes from the fourth chapter: "*Chātur Varnyam mayā srishtam guna karma Vibhāgashah.*"'

'Exactly,' said Govind, 'that means the four-fold division of society was established by Krishna based on *Guna* (nature or constitution) and *Karma* (functions) of individuals. For the Brahmins the mouth was important for teaching and chanting the *mantras* for various rituals; the Kshtriyas used their arms for defending the community from its enemies; and the Vaishyas needed their legs for tending cattle, for farming and for transporting goods for trade. Lastly the Shūdras—artisans—served the other three varnas just as the feet serve the rest of the body.'

'Who made these rules or laid down the guidelines?' asked Vasant.

'The writers of the various *Smriti* texts,' said Govind.

'That means Brahmins. No wonder they kept the power in their own hands!'

'Far from it, Vasant; real power comes from money and political control, but the Brahmins had neither. Brahmins were noted for their "hand to mouth" existence for centuries. The rulers and merchants had real power; the Brahmins were sometimes ministers and advisers, but mainly they were concerned with the preservation of knowledge, teaching philosophy, law, medicine and other subjects, and conducting various rituals.'

'Uncle Govind,' asked Ramesh, 'why were these duties and occupations assigned to particular varnas?'

'Because of their nature; each varna was, by nature, best fitted to perform its particular functions. People are endowed with various talents and it was laid down that the different varnas would best serve society by each following its particular set of duties—*Dharma*. Indians have always assumed that different people have different qualities and individuals of similar qualities are grouped into the same varna. This happens in other societies as well. In the distant past the division of functions was not rigid, because we read in the *Manu Smriti* that a Brahmin, if unable to follow his varna occupation, was allowed to maintain himself by following Kshtriya or even Vaishya occupations. Similarly, a Shūdra was allowed to follow Vaishya occupations.'

'But when and how did the strict separation of different occupations come about?' asked Vasant.

'As Govind has said,' replied Gopāl, 'the varna classification was divine in origin, but not the divisions based on occupation, that is, the jāti classification. The jāti duties became absorbed into varna duties and so individuals were unable to change their occupations, because they had become hereditary in different families. Sons followed their fathers' occupations, and, in most cases, heredity and environment combined to produce children similar in nature to their parents. Thus birth became more and more important in determining varna and jāti. The whole system became stagnated, there was no mobility and, as a result, some had many privileges and others came to be oppressed.'

'Because of the new laws,' said Vasant, 'Brahmins are now suffering oppression.'

'The only remedy is for Brahmin boys to change their occupations,' said Gopāl. 'In Britain, we are told, there is no caste system, and for most individuals it is true, but the best jobs still go to those from certain families and certain schools and universities.'

'But, Uncle Gopāl,' asked Vasant, 'why do Hindus still accept the jāti and varna classification based on Birth?'

'Because people *are* different, and the individual's social position enables him or her to fit into the social structure following an occupation best suited to his or her nature. Besides, one's birth depends on one's Karma, and therefore it is not imposed by society but earned by the individual. It is important, however, that there should be equality of opportunity, not just for scheduled castes, but for all. So the opportunity should be based on personal qualifications and potential and not on jāti.'

'Vasant,' said Govind, 'you were lucky to get admission to a commerce college, but when Ramesh passes his secondary school certificate examination he may fail to get admission to a college because of his Brahmin varna. So he will have to think of joining the armed forces.'

'But what if I fail the physical?' asked Ramesh.

'Then, my son,' said Gopāl, 'you will have to open a shop and follow a Vaishya occupation. That is the only way of removing the varna and jāti differences from our society, and that will perhaps achieve success in an area in which the Law has failed in the last 40 years since independence.'

As a result of the long discussion with his father and uncle, Vasant made a vow to himself that he would pass his degree examination with a good class which would enable him to become a bank manager. His Diwāli vacation was almost over and he left for Bombay the day after Ābā returned from his pilgrimage, towards the end of the fourth week in *Kārtik*.

Ābā had enjoyed the effort of the pilgrimage but on his return journey he had sprained his ankle and therefore had travelled back by bus. Ājī most anxiously went to the front door as Ābā got down from a motor rickshaw, his right ankle bandaged. He reassured Ājī that there was no fracture and that he would be alright in a week or so.

That evening he took out from his bag some boiled sugar discs and roasted chickpeas which had been offered to Vithobā at Pandharpūr and received back as *prasād* (blessed offering). He distributed them to everyone in the family and to his neighbours on either side. Ābā was glad that Vasant was able to receive prasād before he returned to college in Bombay.

'This will bring you good luck,' Ābā said, as he gave prasād to Vasant.

The next morning Vasant was ready for his long distance bus journey to Bombay. He offered namaskār to the family deities and to the six elders in the family, receiving blessings in return from his grandparents, parents, uncle Gopāl and aunt Rādhā. As he picked up his bag and got into the motor rickshaw, Ramesh decided to accompany him as far as the bus station. Amidst all the goodbyes, they set off.

Later that day, Ābā's ankle was still a little bit tender. He was sitting down to tie a new bandage around it when Gitā and Tārā came in. They were eager to find out more about Vithobā.

'Ābā,' said Gitā, 'Vithobā is really Vishnu, isn't he? Are there any other big temples of Vishnu apart from Pandharpūr?'

'Yes, but he is known by his other names. There are temples at Dwārkā and Mathurā dedicated to Krishna, who is really Vishnu. The temples of Jagannāth at Puri, Venkatéshwer at Tirupathi, Varadarāj at Kanchipuram, Shri-Ranga at Shirangapattan, and Padmanābh at Trivendram are all dedicated to Vishnu.'

'Ābā,' said Tārā, 'we have a Vishnu temple here at Wāi. Why do you walk such a long distance to Pandharpūr if Vithobā is really Vishnu?'

'Tārā, my dear, it is true that an image of the same God exists in the Vishnu temple here at Wāi, but each place is different and by going on a *Yātrā* (pilgrimage) we have a chance to see different parts of our country and meet Hindus from those places.'

As Āba finished explaining why he had gone on the second pilgrimage to Pandharpūr, the postman arrived with an airmail letter. Ābā dismissed the girls.

'You had better go and sort out your books for your lessons at school,' he told them.

They walked over to the door leading to the middle room, but Gitā turned round.

'Who is the letter from?' she asked.

'Your aunt Neelā. Now go on, get your books ready.'

Left in peace at last, Ābā opened the letter and was soon engrossed in reading what his daughter had written all the way from Britain.

9

Hindus in Britain, the Thread Ceremony, Āshramas

Now it was *Mārgashīrsha*, the ninth month of the Hindu year and, as the cold season had set in, woollen garments such as pullovers, caps and scarves were in evidence. Although the temperature was only about 40°F, it represented a drop of 50 degrees from the summer temperature, and because of stone floors, unglazed windows and lack of indoor heating, it felt very cold.

After his early morning ginger-flavoured tea and a warm bath, Ābā put on his dhoti, shirt and sleeveless pullover and, wrapping a scarf around his neck, began to read, for the second time, his daughter's letter as he sat in the front room.

Leicester, England

My dear Ābā,

I hope you received my last letter in which I described a religious ceremony of conversion to Hinduism. I hope you all celebrated the *Diwāli* festival for the full five days. Living in Britain has many material advantages and we live in comfort, even in luxury, compared to many middle-class families in India, but we are not able to follow many Hindu rituals or celebrate our festivals to the full. Just to give you an idea, I am going to describe how the majority of Hindus celebrate *Navarātri* and *Diwāli* in Britain. A friend of ours spent last month in the United States and was able to join in the *Diwāli* celebrations which many Hindus had organised in a suburb of New York. His account confirms our experience in Britain.

We do not have a well equipped household shrine here, such as you have in Wāi, and that makes it impossible for me to hang a string garland of marigolds for nine days or keep an oil lamp burning constantly, especially when we are out during the day and Sheila is at school. I offer flowers every day to an image of *Pārvati* and light a lamp during the evenings of *Navarātri* when we are at home. We are able to visit a temple here where *Durga-pūjā* is performed, followed by a *prasād* dinner. There is a large Gujrati community here; they hold stick-dance sessions every evening in the temple hall during the *Navarātri* festival. Ganesh and I have gone to these dances a couple of times but we send Sheila along with her friends for an hour or so every evening.

This year we went to London to take part in the *Dasserah* celebrations which a Hindu temple had organised in a public park in North London. The usual exchange of *Ashmantaka* leaves was not possible on this day, but the gathering had been arranged on the lines of an English country fair with food stalls, side shows and games for children. It was a most enjoyable occasion where we made new friends and it was a dry, sunny day which was a blessing.

When we celebrate *Diwāli*, it is usually an evening get-together for an Indian meal in a public hall hired for the purpose. We light small coloured candles instead of the usual oil lamps and, if there is an open space in front of the hall, children play with sparklers and small fire-crackers. Of course, Ganesh and I offer worship to Laxmi on the *Laxmi-pūjan* evening at home. I do not spend a lot of time preparing special dishes for *Diwāli*, because there are excellent Indian shops here where we can buy *Pedhās*, *Burfee*, *Lādoos*, *Jilébee*, *Mysore Paak* and *Chivadā*. The quality of these sweets is superior because of the select ingredients available.

From what our friend told us about his experience of *Diwāli* in New York, their celebration was not greatly different from ours, except for the fact that a number of people had travelled over 200 miles by car to be present for the occasion. Because of the size of the United States, Asians are not concentrated in small areas, so they have to travel long distances to attend various Hindu festival celebrations. In Britain, on the other hand, large Hindu populations are found in London, Leicester, Birmingham, Manchester and Bradford.

In British schools, children are taught about Hinduism, Judaism, Islam, Buddhism, Sikhism and Christianity, and, with regard to Hinduism, Sheila comes home with incorrect information which her teacher has been giving out. Only last week, her teacher told the class that the Hindu festival of *Diwāli* celebrates Rāma's return to Ayodhyā from his 14 year long exile, when the citizens of Ayodhyā illuminated the capital by lighting thousands of lamps. As you know, *Diwāli* has no connection with the Rāma story, yet some teachers tend to present that story as a dramatic event to celebrate *Diwāli*. They have obviously got confused information about *Rāma-Leelā*, which is celebrated in North India during the *Navarātri* festival. Last week Ganesh and I spent over an hour explaining to Sheila that *Diwāli* celebrates Vishnu's victory over the Demon Narakāsura and King Bali and that special pūjā is offered to Laxmi, the Goddess of wealth and good fortune at the end of the Hindu financial year.

Hindus in Britain face a serious problem concerning the cultural identity of their children born in this country. Very few parents make the effort to teach their children to read and write their mother tongue, or pass on the religious traditions. And yet these children have learned to absorb knowledge from books and it is easy to buy suitable books on Hinduism for them. Only recently have Hindu authors begun to write books for publication by British publishers. These have been very useful and we always buy them for Sheila as presents.

We have been invited to attend a Hindu wedding next month and I shall write to let you know how it is celebrated in Britain.

Has Govind ever performed a ceremony converting a non-Hindu to Hinduism? I hope he found my last letter interesting.

We are all in good health. Convey my namaskār to Ājī, Govind, Yamū, Gopāl and Rādhā. Blessings to Vasant, Gitā, Ramesh, Tārā and Leenā.

With regards.

Your affectionate daughter,
Neelā

Ābā felt a little sad that his British born granddaughter Sheila was not going to experience the Hindu way of life to the full, but he comforted himself with the thought that her parents were able to give her the material comforts and education which his three granddaughters in Wāi were not able to enjoy. A dilution of the religious experience was the price Ganesh and Neelā were prepared to pay in order to enjoy an affluent lifestyle.

Two days later the Wāiker family received a personal invitation from a Brahmin couple to attend their son's *Upanayana*—thread ceremony. The couple also left a printed invitation card giving the exact day and time when the ceremony would take place. That evening Gitā and Tārā read the printed card and asked Ājī whether they would be allowed to attend the ceremony towards the end of the month.

'Of course, Gitā. You, Tārā and Leenā are also invited. We shall all go and witness the ceremony.'

'Ābā,' said Gitā, 'why is it that only boys undergo the thread ceremony?'

'At present, only boys have the *Upanayana* ceremony, it is true; but in the past, when girls did not marry until they were in their twenties, they also had the thread ceremony performed for them. Later, when girls were married when they were 15 or 16 the marriage ceremony replaced the thread ceremony. These days, girls don't marry so young, therefore it is true that they should also have the thread ceremony.

'The *Upanayana* is an initiation *samskāra*—sacrament—to enable a boy to start his study of the scriptures. He becomes eligible to perform various religious rituals and ceremonies. There are three important rituals in the ceremony. The boy is taught to recite the *Gāyatri* Hymn:

"*Aum bhūr bhuvah swaha.
Aum Tat Savitur Varényam bhargo
devasya dheemahee. Dhiyo yo nah
prachodayāt.*"
("We meditate upon the most radiant lustre of the
sun God, who sustains the Earth, the Heaven and
the space between. May he stimulate our intellect.")

'The second important ritual is called *Anjali-Kshāran*. This is performed to purify the boy and propitiate the Sun God. The Priest pours water from his hands onto the boy's hands and the water is allowed to trickle to the ground. He then prays to the Sun and Agni so that they may accept the boy as a disciple worthy of protection and long life.

The third important ritual occurs after the singing of auspicious songs, when the Priest looks at the boy's face, the boy offers *namaskār*—salutation—and receives advice from the Priest.

The *Upanayana* ceremony is described here in detail since it is an important sacrament:

1 *Pūrvānga-Kritya*: This has to be performed prior to *homa* (sacred fire worship), and it has seven rituals. They involve absolution from the fault of not performing childhood *samskāras*; gaining the capacity to perform the *Upanayana Samskāra*; shaving the boy's head; a ritual bath for the boy; offering of *dakshinā*—a cash gift—to the astrologer; auspicious songs; and looking at the boy's face by the Priest. Cash gifts are given to the Priest to obtain absolution for faults.

2 *Pradhāna-homa* (sacred fire oblations): The reason for *homa* is to enable the boy to acquire the capacity to study the *vedas*. Worship is offered to Agni for protection, health and long life. The boy is given a strip of silk cloth to wear as an undergarment, which means that he has to keep his senses under control. He is also given a dhoti to cover his body below the waist, and an upper garment. A piece of deer-skin on soft cotton is tied around his neck. After reciting the *Gāyatri* Hymn ten times, the sacred thread is placed around the boy's left shoulder; the sacred thread is supposed to destroy ignorance and increase understanding.

3 *Anjali Kshāran*: This is done for ritual purification of the boy. The Priest prays to Sūrya (Sun), Agni (Fire) and Prajāpati (the Lord) to protect the boy and grant him long life.

4 *Hridayālambhan*: The Priest touches the boy's heart (chest) indicating that the boy is now qualified to study the Scriptures.

5 *Prathama-Agni-Kārya*: Small sticks of wood are offered to the fire; special prayers are said for keen perception, understanding and intellect. Ash is collected from the fire and smeared on the boy's forehead; he offers prayers for long life.

6 *Gāyatri Upadésh* (*Gāyatri* Hymn): The boy kneels on his right knee before the Priest (or his father) and, touching the Priest's (or father's) right leg from the knee downwards, asks to be given a lesson in the correct pronunciation of the *Gāyatri* Hymn. He then puts his hands together and places them on his right knee, the right hand above the left. The Priest covers the boy's hands with a cloth and recites the Hymn slowly to enable the boy to repeat it. In some families, a cloth is draped over the Priest and the boy while the Priest whispers the Hymn in the boy's right ear.

7 *Deeksha-Pradān*: A string of grass is wound round the boy's

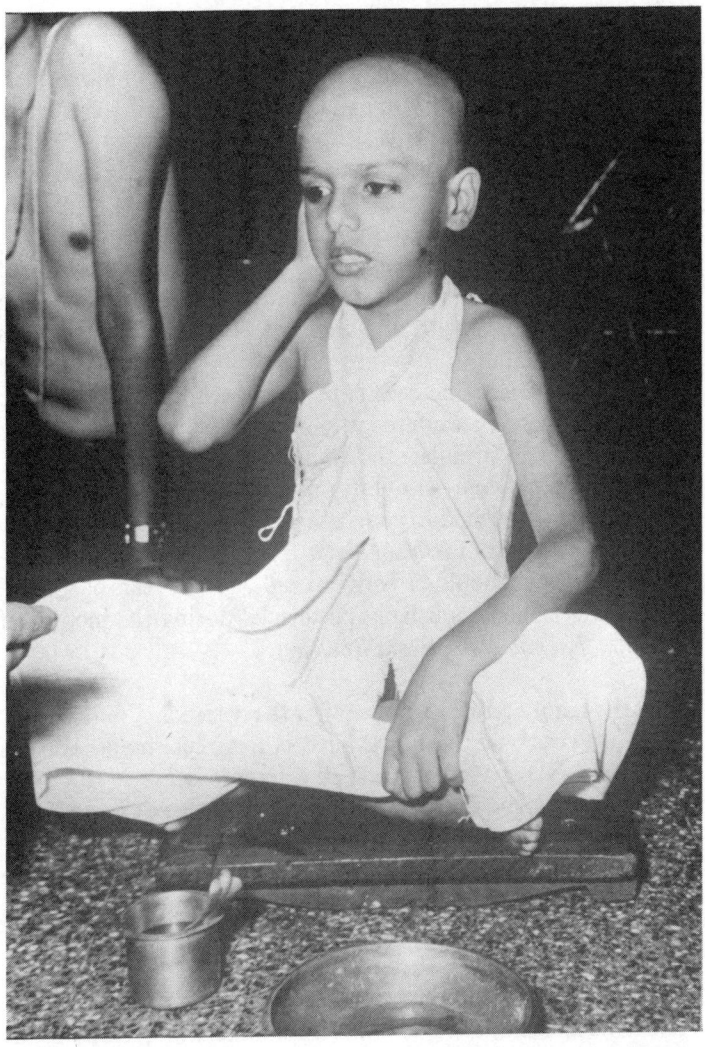

The Thread Ceremony   *Photograph: V P (Hemant) Kanitkar*

waist three times and tied in front. Now the boy is bound to obey the Priest (or teacher) and concentrate on his studies. The boy is given a staff to enable him to follow the right path in his studies. He is advised by the Priest to keep himself clean, offer daily oblations to the Sun, not to sleep during the day, to obey his teacher, offer worship to Agni, study hard for at least 12 years to complete his course and beg cooked food to maintain himself. Once more worship is offered to Agni.

8 *Anupravachaniya Homa*: This Agni worship is performed after the evening oblations to the Sun have been offered. The main prayer is for wealth and intellect. The *Gāyatri* Hymn is chanted at the end.

9 *Medhā Janana*: The Sun is propitiated in order to increase intelligence. Worship is offered to a living branch of a *palasha* tree; this is supposed to stimulate the brain. Prayer is offered for a keen intellect. *Medhā Sūkta*—a hymn praising intellect from the *Rig Veda* appendix is recited to conclude the *Upanayana Samskāra*.

The *Grihya Sūtra* of *Ashwalāyana* says that for the three twice-born *varnas*, boys should be between eight and 12 years of age and the thread ceremony is usually performed during the months of *Vaishākh*, *Jyeshtha*, *Māgh* and *Phālgun*.

When the family returned home after the ceremony, Gitā spoke.

'Ābā, why can't we three girls have a thread ceremony? You did say that girls should also have such a ceremony.'

'I think it is a good idea, Gitā, but this must be discussed with everyone in our family.'

As Ābā promised to discuss Gitā's idea, he felt that perhaps the thread ceremony of the three girls at the same time would bring a little excitement to the town.

The faith of the Hindus is referred to as *Sanātana-dharma*, an ancient way of life, or the *Varna-Āshrama-dharma*, a way of life based on *Varna*—social class—and *Āshrama*, the stage of life.

Hindus assume the human life span to be 100 years; various *mantras* of blessing contain the words '*Jeeveta sharadah shatam*'—'May you live a hundred autumns'. These *mantras* occur in the later books of the *Rig Veda* and the *Grihya Sūtras* of *Ashwalāyan*; which suggests that the ancient Hindus enjoyed long life but perhaps '100 autumns' was wishful thinking. The average life span of the Indian people gradually dropped because of tropical disease, increasing population, infant mortality, and many battles; at the turn of this century it was no more than 30 years. In spite of these conditions many people from the upper *varnas*, who observed strict rules about pollution and diet, lived to be 80, 90 or even 100 years old. Since Independence in 1947, although the population has vastly increased, because of better health care and a reduction in smallpox and malaria, increased food production and a higher personal income, the Indian life span has increased; but it is still nowhere near the European norm.

We have already seen that Hindu society was divided into four *varnas* according to the nature and function of individuals. Traditionally a Hindu's life is divided into four stages called *Āshramas*; and these stages are not of equal length. The first one is *Brahmacharya*—the celibate student stage. The first 12 years of life are childhood, so this first *Āshrama* proper begins with the *Upanayana*—the sacred thread ceremony. Traditionally the various courses involving the study of the vedas, grammar, logic, etymology, literature and poetics lasted for 12 years. This *Āshrama* comes to an end when studies are complete and the young man, in his early twenties, is ready to marry and enter the second stage, which is called *Grishastha-Āshrama*—the householder stage of life.

This *Āshrama* is compared to air which supports life; similarly a householder supports society. Since he has a job, a wife and children and a roof over his head, he can afford a shelter for the needy, fees and books for students, and the care of elderly relatives. He can give alms to religious mendicants and, by paying his taxes, he supports the government indirectly. He can give money to charity and give his time towards some social work. A householder can pursue *Dharma*—moral duty—according to his *Varna*, *Āshrama*, *Kula* and *Jāti*; he can work towards *Artha* (material wealth) and *Kāma* (enjoyment of the objects of the senses), in moderation and always within the bounds of Dharma. *Manu Smriti*—the code of human conduct—says '*Dhanyo Grihasthāshramah*'—the householder stage is indeed the most blessed condition for any man.

The third stage of life is the *Vanaprastha Āshrama*, which is reached when the children are educated and married and a man has secured a pension after a lifetime of employment. All his worldly ambitions, dreams and desires are fulfilled and he has no responsibilities to keep him tied to a grinding routine. As the name of the *Āshrama* suggests, he is free to leave the busy city life and 'retire to a forest'—to be interpreted as 'a place which will give him peace and quiet'—to pursue his hobby, study philosophy, or meditate upon the nature of Brahman—the final reality. Man is reminded that after retirement he is to reduce his material needs, live a simple life, but keep his mind active.

The fourth stage of life is *Sannyāsa*—complete renunciation of the material world, possessions, honours and name. Only a widower without any worldly responsibilities can become a true Sannyāsin, for he must wander from place to place, have very few belongings to enable him to keep body and soul together and beg for his food. A Sannyāsin must spend every waking hour in contemplation of the Supreme Spirit and when he dies there are no cremation rites, because by becoming a Sannyāsin he is already dead to the world. A Hindu Sannyāsin is buried and he has no relation to offer him *pinda* and perform the *shrāddha* ceremony.

Towards the end of the month, Rādhā brought home a weekly newspaper which was published in London and which had been sent to one of the teachers in Rādhā's school by her friend who lived in London. That evening after dinner, Rādhā asked Ramesh and the three girls to come to the middle room to hear an account written in the newspaper article. Govind and Gōpal also joined them and Rādhā began to read it aloud:

A HINDU TEMPLE
by our roving reporter

About a month ago I had a chance to visit a Hindu temple in North London. The temple, which was founded by a devout lady over 30 years ago, is situated in a private house. The front room on the ground floor is converted into a temple and as a visitor enters the front door, there is room to remove one's shoes and keep them safely in the carpeted entrance hall. A door on the right leads into the temple which has a fully carpeted floor, and bright painted walls hung with religious pictures which are illuminated with neon tube lighting.

It is hard to believe that such a holy atmosphere can be created in a private house. There are well-framed pictures of Hindu deities, holy men, Guru Nanak, a statue of Vivekānanda side by side with a plaster relief tablet of Arjuna and Krishna in a chariot. On a glass-fronted cupboard there is a crucifix and near the opposite wall there are two sets of harmonium, brass cymbals and tabla drums which are for *Bhajan*—devotional songs.

Around the two walls are marble statues of Ganesha; Rāma, Laxman, Sitā and Hanumān; Krishna and Rādhā; Pārvati, Santoshi mātā; Durgā riding a tiger; a *shiva-lingam* (the regenerative religious symbol, the phallic emblem of God Shiva); and finally a statue of Shri Sai-Bābā, a holy man from India. Before each image a ghee-lamp and joss-sticks are arranged. Crystal sugar and small pieces of fresh coconut are placed in four metal bowls around the room which the devotees can take as *prasād*. Those who wish to make a cash offering may place their donations in a strong-box. At the far end of the temple, there are comfortable chairs for visitors to enjoy the serene atmosphere.

Visitors are welcome in the evenings and all day on Saturdays and Sundays. A number of Hindu festivals are celebrated throughout the year but the annual Ganesha festival is a unique occasion when over 1000 people attend the *pūjā* and take *prasād*; many people travel from other parts of Britain to be present on this occasion.

I have visited many Hindu temples in different cities in Britain and I think that this particular temple must be one of the best. The temple is also used for celebration of *Satya-Nārāyan pūjā*, religious discourses, *Kirtans*, *Bhajans*, and for secular events such as Indian classical music recitals and meetings to commemorate Hindu saints. A Hindu temple in Britain serves as a focal point for social contacts for the community and, as a Hindu, I am very grateful to the family who run this temple with devotion and efficiency.

'Auntie,' said Gitā, after Rādhā had finished reading the article, '*we* don't see Rāma, Krishna and Shiva in the same temple in India. There are separate temples for these Gods. People who worship Vishnu rarely worship Shiva, yet in this temple in London many different images are kept.'

And Govind said, 'I think it must be difficult outside India to have separate temples for individual Gods. The temple mentioned in the article in fact shows that Hinduism allows people to worship many images of the One God. Many people visit the temple, offer worship to the images of their particular deity, and meet other people. This shows a great tolerance of the faith of other Hindus. I think it is a good idea and perhaps we in India can learn the same tolerance between worshippers of Vishnu, Shiva and Pārvati.

'This temple also seems to put Hindu tolerance for other faiths into practice, since there are pictures and images from both Sikhism and Christianity as well as Hinduism, and these too are respected. This is a very interesting situation. Perhaps Neelā will be able to tell us more about how Hindus in Britain get on with people of other faiths.'

10

A Hindu Wedding, Sankrānti, Hindu Calendar

The month of *Paush*, the tenth month of the Hindu year, almost coincides with January, and on the second day in the light fortnight Ābā received a letter from his daughter Neelā.

Leicester, England

My dear Ābā,
I received your letter soon after *Diwāli*. I hope you have received mine in which I wrote about how we celebrate it here. I am glad to note that Govind found my account of the conversion rituals both interesting and informative. The natural sequel to the conversion of Jean to Hinduism was her marriage to the son of our friends. The marriage took place last month and we attended the wedding ceremony along with 500 other guests, a number of whom were non-Hindus. I made notes of the various stages in a Hindu marriage. Hindus in Britain may not be able to celebrate various festivals to the full, due to different conditions, but they do perform the marriage rituals fully. Of course, every marriage in this country has to be registered at the register office, church or other religious place, so a Hindu wedding ceremony is not sufficient by itself to validate a marriage between Hindus in Britain. I hope you like the detailed account of this particular inter-cultural marriage.

This wedding shows a gradual but very significant change in attitudes of Christians and Hindus in multi-cultural British society. The ceremony consisted of various rituals emphasising important points in a Hindu wedding. Not only was this a union of two families, devout in their own religious traditions, but the occasion showed a happy gathering of two cultures, each side making suitable adjustments and showing great patience so as to understand the other.

Thirteen different rituals were performed. I'll list them for you.

Seemaanta-Pujan: When the bridegroom arrived, he was welcomed by the bride's parents at the boundary of the house where the wedding took place. A red kum-kum mark was applied to his forehead and a ghee-lamp was waved in front of him to ward off evil.

Madhu-Parka: After the welcoming ceremony at the entrance to the hall, the bridegroom entered the building. He was seated on a decorated chair in the *mandap*, where he was offered a welcoming drink—a mixture of milk, ghee, yoghurt, honey and sugar. This ritual is known as the *Madhu-parka*. This is the time when he is given a new set of clothes, traditional or modern, a gold ornament such as a ring, or chain and pendant. He may receive a Rolls Royce or a yacht if his future father-in-law feels in a generous mood, but that is a matter of luck or circumstances rather than custom.

Gauri-Hara-Pūjā: While the *Madhu-parka* ceremony was going on in the *mandap*, the bride offered worship to Pārvati and invoked the Devi's blessing for herself and her future husband. The bridegroom did not see this private meditation and worship.

Anter-pata—Songs of blessings: The bride and bridegroom stood facing each other, on a Swastika design drawn with rice grains, separated by a curtain of silk cloth which was held at each end by the priest and his assistant. On the silk cloth, Swastika and AUM symbols were drawn in red, and the names of the couple were written. The couple could not see each other. Rice grains tinged with red kum-kum powder were distributed among the guests, and specially designed garlands were worn by the couple. Songs of blessing were sung.

As each verse was sung with gusto, the guests held a few grains of rice in their right hands and showered the couple with them at the end of each verse. Each verse ended with the phrase '*Kuryaat Sadaa Mangalam—Shubha Mangala Saavadhaan*'. ('[They] always bring good fortune, therefore welcome this auspicious moment.')

Kanyaa-daan: The daughter—Kanyaa—was formally given in marriage by her father to the bridegroom. Water was poured on the bride's parents' hands which trickled on to their daughter's hands, then on to the bridegroom's hands and finally into a tray which was held by a close relative of the bridegroom. While the water was thus being poured, three generations of ancestors of both bride and groom were mentioned five times by name; the bride's father asked the groom to promise he would be moderate in the observance of *Dharma*, *Artha* and *Kāma*. The bridegroom promised this, three times; he was then given *dakshinā*, a small cash present.

The parents of both parties then stood face to face and held hands, all at the same time, and vowed friendship between the two families. The undertaking was sweetened by the exchanging and eating of sugar. Thus the new family, as a unit, accepted responsibility for the welfare of the new daughter-in-law. At this time the bride was given new clothes and ornaments which will remain her own separate property. These ornaments are known as *Streedhana*. If there are any cash gifts and other presents given after the ceremony, they become the joint property of the couple.

Suvarna—Abhishek: The couple were sprinkled with water from a copper vessel holding gold, signifying the start of a prosperous married life.

A piece of soft cotton, tinged with yellow turmeric, was tied round the wrists of the couple, signifying that they were bound together for life, to the exclusion of all others.

The couple showered each other with blessed rice grains for purification.

Mangal-Sootra (Auspicious necklace): The groom's mother and the groom tied around the bride's neck a necklace of black beads containing a couple of small, open hemispherical pieces of gold, strung on gold wire. This is the emblem of marital status for a Hindu woman. She also wears a small red mark on her forehead during her husband's lifetime. This kum-kum (red powder) and the mangal-sootra are the only ornaments required for the marriage sacrament. But because this was an intercultural marriage, rings were exchanged by the couple.

Vivāha-Homa: Now the couple offered various oblations to the sacred fire while the *Purohita* (Priest) recited the sacred *mantras* in Sanskrit. Oblations were offered to Agni, Prajapati, Indra, Yama, Vaayu, Surya, Chandra, Brihaspati, Maitrā-Varuni, Samudra, Annam, Soma, Savitra, Rudra, Twastrā, Vishnu and Marut, the deities of the *Vedas*. Prayers for worthy children and long life were offered.

Paani-Grahana: The husband, holding his wife's hand, accepted her as his life-long companion.

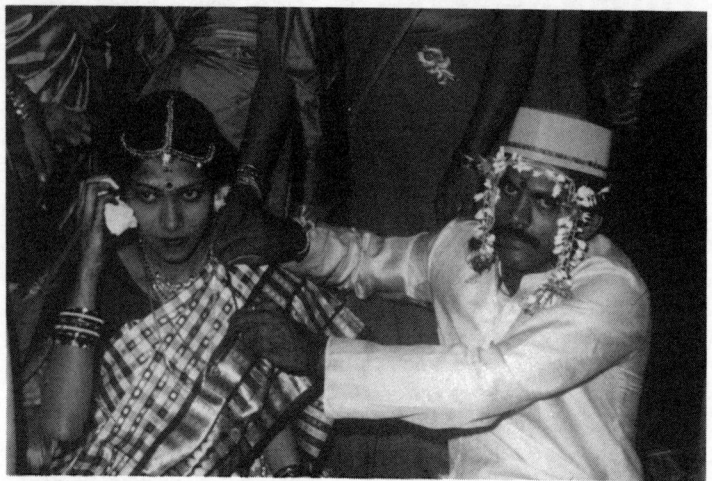

The Mangal-Sootra: emblem of a Hindu woman's marital status

Photograph: V P (Hemant) Kanitkar

Laajā-Homa: The couple offered some roasted paddy or popcorn to the sacred fire.

The brother of the bride pretended to twist the right ear of the bridegroom to remind him of his duty and responsibility towards his bride. The groom promised to do his duty faithfully and gave a small cash present to his brother-in-law. This freed the wife from obligations to her father's family, but now she had obligations to her new family. Both prayed for good fortune and worthy children.

Sapta-Padi: The couple walked seven steps, taking a vow for each step, the wife following the husband. 'Take the first step, *follow me in my vows*. May God be your guide. Take the second step for *power*; the third for *prosperity*; the fourth for *happiness*; the fifth for *children*; the sixth step for the *enjoyment of seasonal pleasures*; and the seventh step for a close union and *life-long friendship*.'

The union becomes indissoluble only after the *Saptapadi* ritual.

Dhruva-Darshan: The couple viewed the Pole-star together. The wife promised to be Dhruva-constant, like the star, in her new family and not to obstruct her husband's good and righteous ventures.

Ashirvaad (blessings): The couple were blessed by the Priest for a long and prosperous married life.

The Pandit went through all the stages that were performed when I married Ganesh in India. The Pandit who performed the ceremony is a learned scholar of Sanskrit and is in great demand among the Hindu community for the performance of various religious rituals.

Please convey my *namaskārs* to my elders, and love and blessings to the youngsters.

Your affectionate daughter,
Neelā

On the Full Moon day of *Pausha*, the Wāiker family got up earlier than usual and everyone had their bodies rubbed with a paste of sesame seeds before the morning bath. A handful of sesame seeds was thrown in the bath water and afterwards the family ate a few seeds and then enjoyed a piece of *burfee*—sweets—made from roasted sesame seeds, dry copra and raw sugar. When the children went to school they took some sesame sweets with them to give to their teachers and friends.

In the evening, married women from a few neighbouring houses were invited to the Wāiker household and anointed with red kum-kum and turmeric powders; they were given a small, unglazed earthen pot filled with wheat and the sesame sweets. Their menfolk also came to receive the sesame sweets and, a little later, Ābā, Govind, Gopāl and Ramesh visited their neighbours to receive sweets too.

'Uncle Govind,' asked Tārā after the evening meal, 'why is this day called *Makara-Sankrānti?*'

'Because on this day the Sun enters the Zodiac sign of *Makara* (Capricorn); this day always falls on 14 January. Now the Sun begins to move northwards.'

'But, Uncle,' interrupted Tārā, 'we have learned in our Geography lessons that the Sun remains in one place and the planets move around it.'

'You are right, Tārā. The sun does stay in one place, but because of the movement of the earth, it appears to move northwards. For the next six months the sun will seem to move towards the *Karka-Vritta*—the tropic of Cancer. This period is called *Uttarāyana*.'

Makara-Sankrānti is known as *Lohri* in North India; in South India it is called *Pongal*. The rituals in different parts of India vary, but the significant feature of the day is that it is based on the apparent movement of the sun, while the Hindu calendar is based on the waning and waxing of the moon.

The Hindu almanac is called *Panchāng* because it deals with the way Hindus calculate time with regard to five (*Panch*) subjects (*Anga*). These subjects are *tithī* (lunar day), *vāra* (solar day), *Nakshatra* (Lunar asterisms), *yoga* (the lucky conjunctions of the planets) and *karana*—a special division of the day—of which there are 11 in all.

A *tithī* is a lunar day, which is based on the movement of the Moon, and approximately 30 *tithīs* make a Hindu lunar month. A *tithī* begins at sunrise and lasts throughout the *divasa* (day) and *rātri* (night).

A *vāra* is simply a day as part of a week. A long time ago Hindus had a five day week, but from AD third century, Hindus began to use a seven day (*saptāha*) week and each day is named after the presiding planet as was the case in ancient Greece.

The Hindu days are: *Ravivāra* (Ravi = Sun), *Somavāra* (Soma = Moon), *Mangalvāra* (Mangal = Mars), *Budhvāra* (Budha = Mercury), *Guruvāra* (Guru = Jupiter), *Shukravāra* (Shukra = Venus), and *Shanivāra* (Shani = Saturn). Out of these, *Magalvāra* and *Shanivāra* are considered unlucky.

A *rāshi* is a house or sign of the Zodiac; there are 12 *rāshis*: *Mesha* (Ram), *Vrishabha* (Bull), *Mithuna* (Couple), *Karka* (Crab), *Simha* (Lion), *Kanyā* (Daughter), *Tulā* (Weighing scales), *Vrischika* (Scorpion), *Dhanu* (Bow), *Makara* (Indian crocodile), *Kumbha* (Water vessel) and *Mīna* (Fish).

A solar year is divided into 12 signs of the Zodiac. The sun passes through 12 *rāshis* in one *vatsara* (solar year) and two and a quarter *nakshatras* each month.

A lunar month is divided into 27 mansions or asterisms called *nakshatras* which are a small cluster of stars lying in the path of the Moon. The Moon passes through the sky in one month moving through a little over one *nakshatra* each solar day. The full Moon each month is in a different *nakshatra*. The 27 asterisms are: *Ashwinī, Bharanī, Krittikā, Rohinī, Mrigashiras, Ārdrā, Punarvasu, Pushya, Ashleshā, Maghā, Purva-Phālgunī, Uttār-Phāl-*

guni, Hasta, Chitrā, Swāti, Vishākha, Anurādha, Jyeshthā, Mūla, Purvā-Āshādhā, Uttarā-Āshādhā, Shravan, Dhanishthā, Shatatārakā, Purvābhādrapadā, Uttarābhādrapadā, Revati. The *Abhijit* asterism makes up the balance.

The Hindu lunar months are *Chaitra, Vaishākh, Jyestha, Āshādhā, Shrāvan, Bhādrap'd, Ashwin, Kārtik, Margashirsha, Pausha, Māgha* and *Phālgun*. The Hindu calendar year begins with *Chaitra* (March–April) but the financial year begins after the *Laxmi-pūjā* evening on the first day of *Kārtik* (October). The names of the months are taken from those of the *nakshatras*. Each month is divided into a *Shukla* (light) and *Krishna* (dark) *Paksha* (fortnight). *Amāvāsyā* is the darkest night and *Paurnimā* is the night of the full Moon. In South India, Bengal and Mahārāshtra, the lunar month begins after *Amāvāsyā*, but in North India and Andhra Pradesh it starts after *Paurnimā*.

There are six *ritus*—seasons—in the Hindu calendar; they are *Vasanta* (spring) during *Chaitra-Vaishākha* (March–April); *Grīshma* (summer) during *Jyeshtha-Āshādha* (May–June); *Varshā* (rains) during *Shrāvan-Bhādrap'd* (July–August); *Sharad* (autumn) during *Ashwin-Kārtik* (September–October); *Hemanta* (winter) during *Margashirsha-Pausha* (November–December); and *Shishira* (cool season) during *Māgha-Phālgun* (January–February).

The equivalent English months do not always coincide with the Hindu seasons because of the five and a quarter days difference between the two calendars. This difference is made up by inserting an additional or repeat month called *Adhika-Māsa* in the Hindu year. This adjustment is made every few years but *Makara-Sankrānti* always coincides with 14 January.

11

Philosophy, Modern Movements, Mahāshivarātri

In the first half of *Māgh*, the eleventh month of the Hindu calendar, the people of Wāi enjoyed a rare treat. The celebrated scholar Dr Shankarrāo Pātil, from a Southern Mahārāshtra university, had been invited to deliver the 'Rāmdās Memorial Lectures' on Hindu philosophy to commemorate the saint-poet Rāmdās who had lived in Western India during the late seventeenth century. The lectures were to take place in the hall of the town's Tilak Memorial Library, and the members of the managing committee personally invited prominent Hindus from all walks of life for the programme. Ābā, Govind and Gopāl decided to attend all the lectures given by this visiting scholar.

Dr Pātil began by saying that in the second half of the twentieth century, the Hindu way of life was in great danger from other religions and the only way of preserving it was, not through aggression, but through self examination, self criticism and streamlining.

'Ladies and Gentlemen, our social institutions must be modernised, and a lot of dead wood thrown away; but in our enthusiasm we must not forget our worthwhile traditions, our ancient literature and philosophy, classical poetry and drama. I am going to outline the six *Darshanas* or systems of Hindu philosophy and speak of the ancient scholars who preached them. In my second lecture, I shall summarise modern movements in Hinduism and in the third, discuss the contributions of many prominent Hindus.

'I shall begin with the *Nyāya* (Logic) system, the first in a series of systems using criticism and analysis which offer an explanation of the universe and also a method of salvation. The *Nyāya* discusses the problem of knowledge and analyses the different ways in which we acquire knowledge. These are: intuition (*pratyaksha*), inference (*anumāna*), comparison (*upamāna*), and verbal testimony (*shabda*). *Pratyaksha* originally implied understanding by means of the senses, but later included all understanding, whether through the senses or not. Two kinds of perception were noted: *Savikalpa* (knowledge about an object) and *Nirvikalpa* (acquaintance with an object).

'Inference operates only with regard to things that are doubtful. It reaches a conclusion by observing the two properties of any subject which are constantly seen together, such as fire and smoke. If we see smoke we infer that there is fire. Inferential reasoning is based on proposition, reason, example, application and conclusion.

'By means of comparison we gain knowledge of an object from its similarity to another object with which we are already familiar. This argument involves knowledge of the object to be understood (say, a wild ox) and perception of similarity ('like a cow'). The *Nyāya* system holds that verbal testimony (*shabda*) denotes an individual, a form, a genus, or all these. We discover the truth of our ideas by the test of action.

'The individual self or soul is real and possesses the qualities of knowledge, feeling, desire and aversion. It is separate from the body, the senses and the understanding. In each individual it is unique and distinct, although there is an infinite number of souls. To the *Nyāya* philosopher, ignorance is the cause of suffering, and only logical explanation can bring release and the achievement of *Moksha*.

'The most important thinker of the *Nyāya* school was Gautama (not the Buddha) who probably lived between the second century BC and the AD first century. Valuable commentaries on the *Nyāya Sutra* are by Vatsyāyana (AD fifth century), Vāchaspati (AD ninth century) and Jayanta (AD tenth century).

'The next school of philosophy, called the *Vaisheshika*, deals with the physical nature of the world. Its legendary founder was Kanāda, the 'atom eater' (AD 400), so-called because he attempted to analyse reality into its smallest constituent parts. Although, like the *Nyāya* school, the *Vaisheshika* was originally atheistic, from the fifth century for about 500 years, these two philosophical schools united in putting forward the theory that a Superior Lord (*Paramātman*) organised the elements that constitute the natural world, while not creating them. The *Vaisheshika* doctrine taught that only the *Vishesha* (particular qualities) of the atoms composing the world are capable of giving each item or being true individuality, and distinguishing one from another of the same class. There are six categories (*padārtha*) of objects that can be named: *Dravya* (substance), *Guna* (quality), *Karma* (action, motion), *Sāmānya* (generality), *Vishesha* (particularity) and *Samavāya* (inherence). *Abhāva* (non-existence) was added later.

'This school put forward a theory of physics in the fifth century in which atoms were thought to be eternal and incapable of being split up. Modern physicists also thought that the atom was the smallest particle until Rutherford managed to split it in 1911.

'According to the *Vaisheshika* school, the atoms, governed by an *adrishta* (invisible) force, are to be found in the four substances—air, earth, light and water. They are believed to be everlasting and indestructible, although when in varieties of combination they form different substances. The five incorporeal substances are *Ākāsha* (ether), *Kāla* (time), *Dik* (space), *Ātman* (soul or self) and *Manas* (mind).

'This school of philosophy held that *Dharma* (merit or virtue) is a quality of the self. *Dharma* brings happiness and salvation. *Adharma* (demerit) is also a quality of the self which leads to immorality and misery.

'The *Nyāya* and *Vaisheshika* schools laid down the first rules of conduct and introduced ideas concerning ways of acquiring knowledge. They also elaborated the notions of *Ātman* (self); a Controlling Lord; and *Dharma* and *Adharma*.

'Next we shall turn our attention to the *Sāmkhya* school, the most important system, founded by *Kapila* (sixth century BC). The classic text book, the *Sāmkhya-Kārikā*, commented upon by Ishvara Krishna, was, however, in existence sometime between the AD first and fifth centuries. Other important texts of this school were written between the eighth and seventeenth centuries. They are: *Sāmkhya-pravachana-Sūtra*, *Sāmkhya-tattava-Kaumudi* and *Sāmkhya-vrttisāra*.

'Kapila, the principal philosopher of this school, wrote: "the complete removal of pain is the only goal of mankind". This system enumerates 25 realities; of which the first two, *Purusha* (cosmic spirit) and *Prakriti* (cosmic matter) are the chief, since from their interrelations stem the remaining 23: *Mahat* (cosmic intelligence), *Ahamkāra* (ego), *Manas* (mind), *Indriyas* (ten abstract sense powers), *Tanmātrās* (five subtle elements) and *Mahābhūtas* (the five pure elements—Earth, Water, Light, Wind and Ether).

'*Purusha* is the animating principle of nature, which interacts with *Prakriti*, resulting in material and physical creation and the emanation of mental awareness. Nothing can be created from nothing; everything that is comes from what has always existed; this basic principle of *Sāmkhya* teaching is summed up in the term *Satkārya-Vāda* (causation of being). *Prakriti* has three qualities, or *gunas*: *sattva* (goodness), *rajas* (activity) and *tamas* (ignorance); this concept of *gunas* subsequently became an integral part of Hindu religious belief. The substance of the *Sāmkhya* school had far-reaching and lasting effects on the philosophical teachings of Hinduism, and its tenets are found in *Tantric* and *Purānic* scriptures, as well as the *Mahābhārata* and the laws of *Manu*. According to *Sāmkhya* philosophy, causes of human suffering may be internal (bodily or mental illness), external (accidents) or supernatural. There is much in common with Buddhist teaching; for example, rejection of animal sacrifice, ideas relating to suffering, and the continuing "creation" process in nature.

'You must remember that Hinduism rejects no way of worship or philosophical interpretation,' continued Dr Pātil. 'The first three philosophical systems became a basis for the next three, and we shall see how the *Yoga* system used *Sāmkhya* ideas to develop its theory and practice. The word *Yoga* comes from the Sanskrit root *yuj*: "to yoke", "to bind together".

'Yoga aims to unite the individual self with the universal spirit—Brahman, and recognises the three-fold classification of pain listed in the *Sāmkhya* system. Yoga aims at freedom from these pains through non-attachment to the world; by physical and mental discipline; and by union of individual soul with universal soul.

'Patanjali, in the second century BC, first codified the system; his *Yoga Sūtra* is the most important text for the school. Vyasa's *Bhāshya* (AD fourth century) is a commentary on the *Yoga Sūtra*.

'Yoga must be learned from a Guru (master) to avoid the physical and moral harm that may occur through over-enthusiasm. *Rāja-Yoga* (kingly yoga) relies on internal discipline to develop the inner power of the mind, while *Hatha Yoga* uses both internal and external disciplines to achieve the final goal.

'The eight aims of Patanjali's course are these:

1 *Yama* (abstentions): Avoidance of injury (*Ahimsā*), lying, stealing, sensuality and greed. These abstentions are intended to reduce and remove desire.

2 *Niyama* (rules to follow): Cleanliness, contentment, self-control, study and devotion.

3 *Āsana*: Balanced posture.

4 *Prānāyāma*: Regularity of breathing.

5 *Pratyāhāra*: The withdrawal of the mind from all sense objects.

6 *Dhāranā*: Concentration.

7 *Dhyāna*: Fixed meditation.

8 *Samādhi*: Trance-like contemplation; a condition from which self-realisation results.

'Patanjali's *Yoga-Sūtra* forms the basis of the philosophy and physical discipline of the Yoga School.

'The main forms of yoga are:

Karma-yoga: liberation through actions.

Jnāna-yoga: liberation through knowledge.

Bhakti-yoga: liberation through devotion.

Mantra yoga: liberation through *mantras*, or meditative prayer.

Laya-yoga: liberation through activation of the body's subtle centres, or *chakras*.

Hathā-yoga: liberation through physical exercise and discipline.

Rāja-yoga: liberation through mental and spiritual discipline; this leads to the highest form of yoga, *Mahā-yoga* (great yoga) or *Rāja-adhirāja-yoga* (king of kings yoga), which involves pure concentrated meditation on the Infinite Reality without the aid of any external or physical exercise or form.

'Each chapter of the *Bhagavadgitā* is called after a yoga, such as *Karma-yoga*, yoga of action; *Bhakti-yoga*, yoga of devotion. The noted *Vedānta* teacher, Shankara (eighth century) preached *Jnāna-yoga* in order to remove ignorance through the practice of *Viveka* (discrimination between the passing and the permanent); *Vairāgya* (withdrawal from the external world); *Shat-sampatti*, control of mind and body; tolerance and contentment; patience, sincerity and constancy; and *Mumukshatwa*, a keen desire for liberation.

'*Hathā yoga* is chiefly based on advice to regulate breathing, the practice of various postures and body purification: it is this form which is widely practised in the West.

'Ladies and Gentlemen, next I shall consider *Pūrva-Mīmāmsā* (reflection, deep thought), which was founded by Jaimini (430–370 BC) and based on his *Mīmāmsā-Sūtras*, which are concerned with ethics. This school is usually referred to as *Mīmāmsā* or *Karma-Mīmāmsā*, because of its emphasis on liberation through action. *Uttara-Mīmāmsā* is called *Vedānta*; this deals with meditation upon Brahman.

'*Shabara Bhāshya*, the outstanding commentary on the *Jaimini-Sūtras*, was composed by Shabara Swāmi (fifth century). There have been many other commentaries and interpretations between the eighth and seventeenth centuries, and it is suggested that *Mīmāmsā* and *Vedānta* are complementary systems.

'*Mīmāmsā* considers the *Vedas* infallible, and that the Vedic language, Sanskrit, is the communicative medium of all creation and of God. Since the words of the *Vedas* are everlasting, the *Vedas* themselves must be everlasting. *Pūrva* (or 'early') *Mīmāmsā* sets out rules for the interpretation of Vedic texts, and includes literary and linguistic analysis. Jaimini held that the main sentences (*Vākyas*) of the *Vedas* contained metaphysical knowledge while the supplements related to reasoning. In his opinion, the *Upanishads* and the *mantras* are *arthavādas*, subsidiary sentences. Shankara (eighth century) maintained, however, that the *Upanishads* were the most important part of the *Vedas*.

'The theme of *Mīmāmsā-Sūtra* is stated concisely in its opening sentence: "*Athāto dharma jidnyāsā* [Now comes the enquiry into duty]." *Dharma* here is taken to mean right, or moral, performance of duty; the underlying principle is that faith without works profits not at all, and that religious knowledge without practical application cannot win liberation of the soul. Through the practice of Vedic ritual, both mind and spirit may be enlightened, and therefore the practical guidance of the *Vedas* is basic to spiritual and intellectual progress towards liberation.

'Like the *Sāmkhya* and *Yoga* systems, *Vedānta* is an important and influential addition to Hindu philosophy. The literal meaning of the term *Vedānta* is 'completion of the Veda' (*anta* = end); this is why the system is sometimes called *Uttara Mīmāmsā*, 'later examination'. It is based on the *Vedānta Sūtra*, or *Brahma Sūtra*, of Bādarāyana (c 200 BC), and the later commentaries upon it by Gaudapāda (c AD 700), and Shankara (AD eighth century) one of the greatest of Indian philosophers. Other major *Vedānta* scholars include Rāmānuja (AD 1040–1137), Mādhava (AD 1199–1260), Rāmakrishna (AD 1834–1886) and Vivekānanda (AD 1863–1902).

'In its teachings the *Vedānta* is closely allied to the *Upanishads*, in the sense that true understanding of the self is held to come through knowledge; fulfilment of ritual practices and other actions are not enough to obtain the soul's release from *samsāra* (rebirth). Brahman, the Supreme and Ultimate Reality, is One, formless and eternal, and the origin of all that is revealed. Man is part of all that exists, and therefore is united with the Real, and at one with it. Man's intellect can never be great enough to comprehend Reality, which is Infinite, and the idea of a personal God, *Ishvara*, in whatever form, is, to Shankara, mere illusion.

'In his commentary *Bhāshya*, Shankara puts forward the doctrine of non-dualism (*advaita*) by which all reality is viewed as one; the individual soul—*ātman*—is thus a part of, and indivisible from, Brahman. The plurality of beings and natural phenomena in the world, and, indeed, the world itself, are but evidences of *māyā* (illusion), and man has to realise this and look beyond it to find the self-realisation that brings release to the soul. Shankara sums up the theory thus: "*Brahma satyam Jagan-mithyā* [Brahman alone is Truth; the world is but illusion caused by *māyā*]."

'The far-reaching influence of Shankara's interpretation of *Vedānta* was helped by his extensive journeying and preaching throughout India, and the establishment of his four widely-scattered *mathas* (centres of religious teaching) at Shringéri, Puri, Badrināth and Dwārkā. His monist interpretation of the *Vedānta* remains the most highly esteemed, but two other commentators deserve particular attention, namely Rāmānuja, founder of Viśishtādvaita, and Mādhava, who developed the *Dvaita* theory.

'*Viśishtādvaita* (modified non-dualism) attempts to deal with some of the inconsistencies inherent in Shankara's philosophy. Brahman and the individual soul, or *ātman*, are presented as separate entities, although the soul is ever-dependent upon Brahman, returning to its source after the final release from *samsāra*. The world was created by the Eternal as a kind of sport (*lilā*); Rāmānuja's theory gives Brahman a personality, thus enabling the establishment of a devotional relationship between man and a personal God (*Īshvara*) through which the soul can ultimately achieve its release. Rāmānuja presented *Vedānta* philosophy in a way more intelligible and meaningful to ordinary people than did Shankara, with his very analytically detached, impersonal and formless concept of the Eternal Reality.

'Mādhava rejected the interpretations of both Shankara and Rāmānuja, and postulated the *Dvaita* theory, by which the Eternal and the ātman are, and always were and will be, separate entities. *Moksha* is not a merging of the soul with God, but a means of approaching God to contemplate and revere the causative principle of creation. Each *ātman* is distinct, and different from all others; although dependent on God, it acts independently and has its own body of responsibility—thus the idea of *Karma* is reinforced. This individuality of action and responsibility enabled Mādhava to be one of the very few Hindu religious teachers to adapt the idea of everlasting damnation for some souls, while others may achieve eternal liberation.'

On the way back from the first lecture in the series, Āba said, 'Dr Pātil is a learned man even though he is not from the Brahmin Varna.'

'But Āba,' said Gopāl, 'he is now a Brahmin because of his scholarship. It is all a matter of opportunity and in new India Brahmins no longer have the monopoly of learning.'

'You are right, Gopāl, and we are fortunate to have these lectures by this 'Modern Brahmin'; but the Brahmin-ness is the result of generations of nurture and tradition.'

The three men walked silently home.

'Ladies and Gentlemen,' began Dr Patil, 'in this second lecture I will talk about modern movements within Hinduism.

'After British rule was firmly established in the early decades of the nineteenth century, Western ideas of individualism, progress, property, rational ethics and nationalism began to filter into Indian intellectual and political life. Indians were influenced by these ideas as well as by Christianity, and to meet this challenge some of them began to re-discover our ancient traditions. Through this rediscovery they were able to reject the claimed superiority of Christianity while examining Western ideas without prejudice. Rām Mohan Roy (1772-1833) led the way for social and religious reform. He worked for the British East India Company as a revenue officer and knew Arabic, Persian, Sanskrit, English, Bengali and Hindi. He retired at an early age and devoted the rest of his life to study and reform. He was influenced by the Unitarians, who were themselves seeking reform in the orthodox Christian church.

'Rām Mohan Roy founded the *Brahmo Samāj* (society) in 1828, which tried to combine the best from India and the West. He studied *Vedānta* doctrine, gave up image worship and, through the Brahmo Society, tried to bring about social and religious reforms. The members of this society were rejected by their families as well as by Hindu society because their mode of worship was similar to Christian practice. The Brahmo Society's work was based on three principles: rational thinking, humanism and social reform, and although Rām Mohan pointed out that these ideals were consistent with the best in Hindu tradition, his inspiration came from Western influence.

'The practice of *Suttee* (widow burning), child marriage and untouchability were the practices he protested against; practices that were picked on by Western critics as serious flaws in Hindu society. Rām Mohan accepted the humanitarian teachings of Jesus Christ without becoming a Christian, but he and his successors—especially the Tagores and Keshub Chunder Sen—always considered *Vedānta* philosophy as the scriptural source and foundation of Hinduism. The Brahmo Society created a rational and critical attitude in many Indian minds, which enabled us to absorb the best from the West without losing our Indian identity.

'If Rām Mohan's inspiration came from Western influence,

Dayānanda Saraswati's (1824–1882) inspiration to found the *Arya Samāj* came from the *Vedas*. Dayānanda was born into a Gujarati family who worshipped Shiva. At an early age he rejected image worship and rituals. He left home to avoid marriage and practised yoga to attain *Moksha*, but he felt that social improvement was as essential as spiritual progress if full human potential was to be realised. He was influenced by *Vedānta* for a few years, then he started his study of the *Vedas* under the guidance of Virjānanda, his teacher, and this formed the basis for the foundation of the Arya Society. He decided that the *Vedas* showed the robust philosophy which was most suitable for Indian society and so he rejected Western ideas as well as *Vedānta*. The Vedic ideal of energetic and organised effort for the good of Hindu society directed Arya Samāj towards social reform and the nationalistic movement. The Samāj worked along the lines of Christian missionaries and placed an emphasis on education and an active, involved lifestyle to help humanity. The mainstream of Hinduism did not oppose the Arya Samāj as it had the Brahmo Samāj, because Dayānanda had found inspiration for his work in the *Vedas*. The Arya Society's ideal is to improve the quality of life in the present rather than worry about *Karma* and *Moksha* in future lives.

'Ladies and Gentlemen, this second lecture was much shorter than the first one and the third one will be equally short but rather important. I look forward to seeing you tomorrow.'

Rādhā had accompanied the men to Dr Pātil's second lecture, and on their return she spoke to her father-in-law, which rather surprised Gopāl and Govind, as it is unusual in a traditional Hindu family for daughters-in-law to address their elder relatives directly.

'Ābā, do you think women have the same right as men to achieve *Moksha*?'

'Yes, I think so,' replied Ābā, unconcerned about her directness. 'The *Bhagavadgitā* pointedly mentions women's right to *Moksha*. Every individual can attain release from the cycle of birth and death by following his or her *Dharma*. As Dr Pātil pointed out in his first lecture, the way of *Yoga* or the way of *Bhakti* are within easy reach of ordinary men and women and one does not have to follow any particular form of worship or visit a temple to be a good

Hindu. It is essential that we follow our own individual *Dharma* to the best of our ability and leave the rest to Pānduranga.'

'Ladies and Gentlemen, as I said yesterday,' began Dr Pātil, 'this third lecture will be fairly short and this evening I shall consider the important contributions of four modern Hindus.

'Gadādhar Chattopādhyāya (1836–1886) was a Bengali Brahmin and worked as a priest at a Kāli temple. From an early age he was able to go into a trance, and was more interested in experiencing God than learning about him from books. He learned the *tāntrik Sādhanās* (magical techniques), yogic practices and a little later *Vedānta*. Through his mystical experience of God he was able to put forward the view that all religions were true; the major religions, Hinduism, Christianity, Islam and Zoroastrianism express the oneness of all things in the Universal Spirit. He held that books on philosophy teach about God, but God-realisation was possible only through intuition, love, faith and surrender. His Guru (teacher) gave him the new name of Rāmakrishna and later his followers added the title Paramahamsa (supremely holy).

'We cannot talk on Modern Hinduism without mentioning Narendranāth Dutt (1863–1902), who was born in Calcutta and graduated from a Christian missionary college. He was well acquainted with Western philosophy. He joined the Brahmo Samāj and met Rāmakrishna in 1882. He was given the new name of Swami Vivekānanda, and after deep study of yoga and meditation, travelled widely in India. In 1893 he represented Hinduism at the Parliament of Religions in Chicago, and after his success there became a Hindu missionary and an expert on *Vedānta*. He favoured material well-being and strength rather than the weakness of *Ahimsā*. He declared that each Soul was potentially divine; the goal was to manifest this inner divinity by controlling internal and external nature. Control can be achieved by yoga, and through the practice of yoga, man becomes free. For Swami Vivekānanda, things like rituals and temples were minor details, and he emphasised that Hinduism was tolerant of other faiths while maintaining its own identity. He established Rāmakrishna Mission, named after his teacher, which now has centres in all parts of the world, rendering service to mankind and fulfilling Vivekānanda's vision of practical Vedāntism.

'No lecture on modern Hinduism would be complete without reference to Mahātmā Gandhi. His life is an open book and I am not going to repeat what you have already read in his writings and in the numerous books about him. Gandhi's political and social activities were governed by the ideals of *Satya* (truth), *Ahimsā* (non-injury) and *Sevā* (service). These three principles are ignored every day by Hindus even now. Our large cities have thousands of men and women living in sub-human conditions. This is a gross violation of *Ahimsā*. Indians produce too many children, which lowers the quality of life for everyone in the family. Our population increases at the alarming rate of 12 million mouths each year, and this 'demon' continues to swallow up our increasing food production, which adds to the problems of poverty and malnutrition. This is certainly against the principle of *Ahimsā*. Hindus must improve the quality of their lives by controlling the population; this would be a true monument to Gandhi.

'Finally, Ladies and Gentlemen, we must remember Dr Sarvepalli Rādhākrishnan (1888–1975), who has made a lasting contribution to the preservation of Indian philosophy through his scholarly writings. He taught philosophy at Madras, Calcutta and Oxford Universities and wrote with authority on Indian philosophy, the *Bhagavadgītā* and the principal *Upanishads*.

'There is another matter which must be mentioned here because it concerns our heritage of temples. Some of you have probably read the article in *The Illustrated Weekly of India* of 1 March 1987, by Subramanian Swamy in connection with the *Bābri Masjid* (Mosque) in Ayodhyā, which was built on its present site after the Shri Rām Janmasthan temple was demolished by order of Bābur in 1528. Since 1950, by a court order, Muslims have not been allowed to go within 200 yards of the mosque, because since December 1949 images of Shri Rāma and other Gods have been installed in the building. That court order is still in force. Now Muslims have undertaken to recover the mosque from Hindus. In this case Hindus must assert themselves and persuade the Muslim leaders to agree to respect the sentiments of believers in the majority religion. Muslims in India are not a threatened minority because Hindus have displayed tolerance towards their faith during our 40 years of independence. We must obtain such an agreement to make our heritage safe. Not only must we, as Hindus, make a positive effort to preserve our religious buildings, philosophy and other religious writing, but we must persuade the minority religions not to destroy them. Hindus must encourage the new generation to study our philosophy and preserve our ancient heritage, without which this world will be a poorer place.'

As Dr Patil finished his third lecture, the Librarian thanked him for reminding the Hindus of Wāi of their ancient heritage, garlanded him, and presented him with a woollen shawl as a mark of respect for his learning. Dr Pātil was accepted as a 'New Brahmin' by the Orthodox Brahmins, an encouraging event showing progress and change in modern Hinduism.

It was during the dark fortnight of the month that Ābā's family observed the fast of *Mahāshivarātri* and offered worship to Shiva.

'Ābā,' said Ramesh, 'you have already told us about the important Vishnu temples in our country. On this day of *Mahāshivarātri*, please tell us something about the Shiva shrines.'

'Well,' began Ābā, 'before the ancient Aryans settled in this country, the original inhabitants used to worship a stone shaped like a *linga* (male sex organ) in their fertility rites. The newcomers adopted this practice and many legends about Shiva were told and written in mythology. Shiva is normally worshipped in the *linga* form. The *lingas* are made of stone, metal, earth or wood. Sometimes a temporary *linga* is made of butter, sandalwood paste or sweetened dough. Highly polished stones found in the bed of Narmadā river are called *Bāna-lingas*.

'There are five *Pancha-bhūta-lingas* (five naturally-formed or elemental *lingas*) at Kanchipuram, Shrirangam, Arunāchalam, Kālahasti and Chidambaram, all in South India. There is a Shiva temple in most towns and villages, but the most important temples are built to house the 12 *Jyotir-lingas* (effulgent *lingas*), and to the worshippers of Shiva these are sacred centres of pilgrimage. They are: *Bhīmā-shankara*, 75 miles from Puné in Western India; *Ghrishnéshwer*, three miles from Devagiri or Daulatābād; *Kedāresh* at Kedārnāth in the Himālayas; *Mahākaleshwer* at Ujjain; *Mallikārjuna* on Mount Shrīshaila in Kurnul;

Nāganāth near Pūrnā junction in Parabhani district; *Omkāra* on the *Narmadā* river in Madhya Pradesh; *Rāméshwaram* at the southern tip of our country; *Somanāth* in Saurāshtra; *Tryambakeshwer* on the *Godāvari* river near Nāsik; *Vaidyanāth* at Parali near Paithan; and *Vishwéshwer* at Banāras or Kāshi.'

'Ābā, have you visited any of these shrines?' asked Ramesh.

'Yes, but only three: the ones near Puné, Nāsik and Daulatābād,' replied Ābā. 'These Shiva temples are situated all over our country, and by going on a pilgrimage one can see different parts of India.'

Govind announced that he was going to keep an all-night vigil at the Shiva temple near the river between sunset and sunrise.

'May I come with you, uncle?' asked Ramesh.

'Yes,' Govind agreed, 'as long as you keep awake all night.'

About half an hour before sunset, Govind and Ramesh went to the temple. Govind brought fresh water from the river and filled the perforated copper vessel that was suspended above the Shivalingam. Water dripped onto the linga-image and Ramesh took it upon himself to keep the vessel full of water so that Govind could recite verses of praise. Every three hours Govind offered *Bilwaleaves* (woodapple leaves) in special worship, uttering Shiva's epithets: *Shiva, Shankara, Sāmba-Sadāshiva, Mahéshwera* and *Rudra*.

When Govind had offered the fifth worship just before sunrise, both of them returned home. No one was surprised to see Ramesh head straight for his bed in the middle room and within ten minutes fall asleep.

12

Cremation, Holi, Village Hinduism

On the third day of *Phālgun*, the twelfth month of the Hindu calendar, Ābā had just finished his morning bath and, after putting on a clean dhoti, was sitting in the household shrine reciting a Sanskrit hymn in propitiation of the planets. Suddenly Rāmji ran into the house calling him.

'Ābā, Ābā,' shouted Rāmji, 'my neighbour needs your help ... he needs your help.'

Ābā interrupted his recitation and came out to the front room.

'What is it, Rāmji?' he asked.

'Ābāji,' panted Rāmji, 'my neighbour's son went out to their field early this morning and he was bitten by a *saap* (cobra). The boy ran back quickly, but did not reach home, because the poison spread very fast. He collapsed in the next street. Some people picked him up and took him to the hospital but the doctor could do nothing. The poor fellow was dead. When they examined his legs, they found bite marks on his right leg, just above the ankle. The leg had turned quite blue.'

'Rāmji, how can I help?'

'My neighbour, Mahādev, does not have much money and the burning will cost a lot. I thought perhaps you could make a small contribution. I can give 20 rupees.'

'How much will the cost of wood fuel and cow-dung slabs be?' asked Ābā.

'I don't know exactly,' said Rāmji, 'but it may be about 70 or 80 rupees.'

'Well, I can give 20,' said Ābā, 'and we'll ask two or three other people for another 40 rupees.'

'Can you come with me now? Mahādev needs our support.'

'Yes. Let me put on my shirt and we shall go.'

When Ābā and Rāmji reached Mahādev's humble home, they heard the women in the house wailing and grieving over the death of the boy. Mahādev sat near the front door, holding his head, tears gently trickling down his unshaven face.

'Mahādev,' said Rāmji, 'look, Ābāji has come. Don't worry. We'll arrange everything.'

Mahādev wiped his face with the end of his dhoti and nodded in silent appreciation of his neighbour's words. Ābā and Rāmji left him and went to see the wood seller about the necessary fuel for the boy's cremation.

'Sadu,' said Ābā to the fuel trader, 'a death has taken place; it is Mahādev's son. We need some wood and cow-dung slabs.'

'How old was the boy?' asked Sadu.

'He was 17 and well built, nearly a man,' said Rāmji.

'In that case you will need the full weight that is usually needed for a grown-up,' said Sadu.

'How much will that be? And would you load up the cart and take it to the burning *ghāt*?' said Ābā.

'I will load up the usual amount, mostly mango-tree, with some cow-dung slabs. It will cost you 80 rupees. You can take some bamboo and string now.'

Ābā and Rāmji collected the bamboo and returned to Mahādev's dwelling where other neighbours had gathered, among them Govind. Govind agreed to perform the last rites and four neighbours promised to pay ten rupees each to make up the cost of the fuel. Ābā, Rāmji and others tied old dhotis around their heads as funeral turbans and prepared the stretcher. A piece of new white cloth was spread on the stretcher and the *preta* (corpse) was bathed and placed on it; another piece of cloth was spread over the corpse but the face was left uncovered. A garland of red flowers was placed around the neck of the body. Mahādev carried live embers in an unglazed earthen pot and walked in front of the procession as the neighbours picked up the stretcher and walked towards the cremation *ghāt*, making sure that the feet of the corpse were pointing in the direction of the journey. Most babies are born head first, therefore the feet of the *preta* (corpse) have to point in the direction of the last journey.

When the funeral procession arrived at the *ghāt*, Sadu was

The scene at a Hindu Cremation Photograph: Ann & Bury Peerless

waiting with the necessary wood fuel. A pyre was prepared by arranging logs in layers so that those in each layer were at right angles to the ones below. When the *preta* was placed on top, its head pointing north, some cow-dung slabs were arranged to cover the head. Govind recited *mantras* to ensure that Agni (fire) would release the soul of the dead by breaking the skull and reducing the earthly remains to ashes. Mahādev lit the pyre with the embers. He pierced a hole in the earthen pot, filled it with water, and walked around the pyre so that the trickling water drew a line on the ground. He went round the pyre three times setting a boundary line with water. He threw the empty pot over his right shoulder towards the south. As a regional variation the chief mourner goes round the pyre three times, holding a burning piece of wood in his hand, thus setting a boundary with a flame. These two rituals are performed to prevent the soul from escaping in a horizontal direction, and to thus encourage it to escape upwards into the atmosphere.

The pyre soon blazed and an hour later, when the skull cracked, Mahādev and the others returned home. The whole family were to remain in mourning for ten days and the ashes were to be collected and thrown into the river on the third day.

After the pollution period of ten days was over, Rāmji and

Mahādev came to see Ābā early one morning. Ābā and his son, Govind, being Brahmins, had performed their morning *Sandhyā*, which involves a purification ritual with water, touching the head, torso, arms and legs while *mantras* are chanted, and offering a water oblation to the Sun while reciting the *Gāyatri* hymn. When Rāmji came, Ābā was sitting in the front room, waiting for a second cup of tea. Ājī brought the tea to the front room, and, seeing the visitors, asked them to wait for a few minutes so that she could offer them some tea as well. After Ājī had brought two more cups of tea and returned to the kitchen, Mahādev spoke.

'Ābā,' he said, 'as you know, I came to live in this town to run a small dairy, but many of my relations still live in our village, about three miles to the west of Wāi.'

'I also come from the same village,' said Rāmji.

'Are you thinking of returning to your village?'

'No, not permanently, but we want to visit the village and see our *Jāti* priest,' said Mahādev.

'Why do you need to see your Jāti priest? I am sure Govind will be able to help,' said Ābā.

'I know,' replied Mahādev, 'but Govind only deals with things which a Brahmin family understands. And we are not Brahmins. Govind does not fully understand how things are done in a village.'

'But you are also Hindus, are you not?'

'Yes, we are,' replied Rāmji, 'but nearly 80 people in every 100 live in villages, and the *Sircar* (Government) papers say that there are over a *lakh* [100 000] villages in our country. Our beliefs and practices are not the same as Brahmins or Vaishyas, even though we are all Hindus.'

'I agree that things are done differently in villages,' said Ābā, 'but why do you need to see your caste priest?'

'Well,' said Mahādev, 'my wife and I are worried about our younger son and daughter. My wife feels that our *Jāti* priest will tell us how to protect them. Will you come to our village, tomorrow? We can start early so that we shall have a whole day to do what needs to be done.'

Ābā agreed to go with them and the three men left for Mahādev's village early next morning. Ābā carried two bananas and some peanuts with him for his mid-day snack, for there were no Brahmin households in the village and he would not be able to accept cooked food from any of the castes there.

After about an hour's walk they approached the village and on its boundary there was a large round stone, painted with red lead oxide. As the men came close to the stone, Rāmji and Mahādev removed their sandals and bowed before it.

'This is one of the *Grāmadevatās*, one of the village gods,' said *Rāmji*, 'that protect the village from evil forces that may come from outside.' Ābā also bowed before the stone, although he could not name the divinity that was present in it for his companions.

'What other *Grāmadevatās* are there in this village?'

'There are *Mari-Āee* or *Mātā* and *Bahirobā* with the *Nandi* (bull) statue in front of its small temple,' said Rāmji.

Ābā assumed that *Mari-Āee* was a Mother Goddess and the other was the village version of Shiva.

'Then there is the Shankara temple in the village square and opposite it there is a Hanumān temple,' continued Rāmji. 'These we call Deva, but we don't think they help the villagers much. As you know there is the annual *Jatrā*—village religious festival—in honour of *Bahirobā*, when many people from surrounding villages attend and offer new clothes to the *Grāmadevatā* to fulfil some vow or other.'

'But at the *Mātā* shrine, in Navarātri,' said Mahādev, 'many people make an offering of a chicken, which is killed in front of the *Mūrti* (image) and used as *prasād*, a sacred offering.'

'Why are the chickens offered to *Mātā*?' asked Ābā.

'In gratitude for a good harvest,' said Rāmji.

They had now reached the village square and Mahādev led his companions to a humble cottage of mud brick with a corrugated iron roof.

'Pānduranga!' called Mahādev. A man of about 40 came out and looked at the visitors. Mahādev and Rāmji explained the purpose of their visit and asked the man to guide them.

'We'll have to see Sītā, who usually helps me,' said Pānduranga, the caste-priest. He sent a message to Sītā, who came after ten minutes. The caste-priest spoke to her privately and she agreed to help. Sītā had brought with her a copper plate on which a Mother-Goddess image was embossed. This was placed on a stone near a wall inside the hut where the priest and the visitors sat. Sītā, who was a slim, middle-aged woman, let her hair down and smeared her forehead with yellow turmeric powder. The priest took out a small drum from an alcove which he began to beat to keep time, and Sitā slowly swayed to the rhythm. The tempo gradually increased and the woman danced energetically, her eyes rolling, her bangles tinkling, while she breathed quickly. After about 20 minutes she collapsed and lay still on the floor. The drum stopped and the four men watched silently. The woman sat up and began to speak.

'The untimely death of your son was caused by the *bhut*—ghost—of your former neighbour's wife who died childless. She was fond of your son before you went to live in the town. Place an offering of boiled rice and yogurt and fried red chillies on a banana leaf at the place where three roads meet. Put a coconut and four green bangles every month before the *Mātā* image for the next five years. The first offering will silence the *bhut* and the second offering to *Mātā* will protect your younger son and daughter.'

Ābā was amazed to see the change in the woman as she came out of the trance and became her gentle self. She drank some water, cleaned her forehead and, wrapping the copper plate in a cloth, left the hut.

'I will ask my wife to cook some rice,' said the caste-priest to Mahādev. 'You go and buy a coconut and bangles from the shop.'

Ābā and Rāmji stayed in the hut while Mahādev bought the offerings. The priest's wife soon prepared some boiled rice and fried red chillies and put the offering on a banana leaf. She then placed the leaf on a tile which Mahādev carried as the priest accompanied him to the crossroads.

The second offering was to be made at the *Mātā's* shrine. This time the priest's wife went with the four men and made the offering on behalf of Mahādev.

'How much money?' asked Mahādev.

'Ten rupees,' said the priest. 'I have to give five rupees to Sitā.'

After Mahādev had settled with the priest, Ābā, Rāmji and Mahādev went to the Shankara (Shiva) temple where they offered homage. Rāmji and Mahādev had also brought a snack with them. The three men ate their food and began their journey back to Wāi.

'Do you think your children will be safe?' asked Ābā.

'Yes, I am sure. The priest said so,' replied Mahādev.

'Ābā,' said Rāmji, 'it is our faith that protects us in the village. The *swamī* (holy man) at Pandharpūr told me that what the Brahmins do, and what the other castes do in the villages, taken together, makes our *Hindu-dharma*. The devas like Vishnu, Shankara, Ganesh and Hanumān, as well as the *Grāmadevatās*, are all included in our *dharma*—religion.'

Ābā had to agree with Rāmji.

'Ābā,' said Mahādev, 'I am glad that you and Rāmji came with me. I am also glad to have made the two offerings. Now my son's *ātmān* (soul) will find peace; perhaps he will be born again as a man.'

'Why do you say that?' asked Rāmji.

'Because he harmed no one. He was a good boy.'

They reached the town, and as Ābā walked towards his home in the afternoon he felt that he was beginning, for the first time in his life, to understand the strong faith held by those involved in the simpler side of the Hindu religion.

On the Full Moon day of the month, the Hindus of Wāi, along with those in thousands of villages, celebrated the festival of *Holi*. *Holi* is a spring festival, and if we remember that spring and autumn are the two harvest seasons in India, we can appreciate its carefree character at a time when the harvest is safely gathered in and the hearts of the farming population of India are for a time sufficiently relieved from anxiety over food to permit abandonment to feasting and merriment. The harvest season is a festive one not only among the rural population of India but among farmers of every country.

Govind had lit the *Holi* bonfire before the mid-day meal and offered worship in the form of milk and the stuffed chapati oblations. At the end of the *pūjā*, Ramesh made Tārā and Leenā giggle by blowing a conch shell. Normally, men and boys make a peculiar sound by shouting and striking their open mouths with the backs of their right hands.

After lunch, Ramesh and Govind went out to organise the neighbourhood *Holi* bonfire for that evening. Many boys in the locality were only too eager to visit each household and collect fuel for the bonfire. This fuel included logs of wood, broken pieces of furniture, old newspapers and a few slabs of dried cow-dung. The bonfire was erected at the crossroads and lit as soon as it was dark. Govind offered *pūjā* again and many people—men, women and children—threw either some rice or a small coin into the bonfire. They went round it in a token gesture of reverence and streaked their foreheads with the ashes for good luck.

The next day, children and grown-ups enjoyed themselves by playing with coloured water. Gitā, Tārā and Leenā used metal syringes to squirt the coloured water at people from a distance, and they rather enjoyed spraying Ābā, Govind, Gopāl, Ramesh, Yamū, Rādhā and even Ājī. After about three hours of colourful nonsense and frolicking, when the coloured ammunition was used up, the children called it a day, bathed, and changed into clean clothes. The Holi festival was over, and in a fortnight's time the new year would begin.

Three or four days after Holi, Ābā received a letter from Neelā in England.

Leicester, England

My dear Ābā,

In my previous letters I mentioned how Hindus celebrate *Diwāli* and other festivals in Britain and how a Hindu marriage is performed here. Although the festivals are celebrated in an abbreviated form and not always on the exact day, the celebration of the thread ceremony and marriage takes place on auspicious days and the important stages are performed very accurately.

The different environment, lifestyle, climatic conditions and food have certainly affected the ritual purity of our lives. For example, in the winter it is inadvisable to take a bath before the morning *pūjā* and then go out into the cold atmosphere. I have a good wash, wash my feet and then perform *pūjā* on weekdays. At the weekend, a bath before performing *pūjā* is practicable because both Ganesh and I have no office work and Ganesh does the supermarket shopping on Saturday mornings. We go together to an Indian grocer.

In many Hindu families, children born here do eat meat and although meat may not be actually cooked in the kitchen, food containing meat or eggs is bought from supermarkets and consumed in the house, thus our ritual purity is affected.

There are many Hindu temples in Britain and, generally speaking, greater ritual purity of atmosphere is to be found in the temples than in Hindu homes. Although new forms of ritual pollution through meat, eggs and alcohol have entered our homes, the traditional sources of pollution, namely birth and death, are practically non-existent in our homes, since they usually take place in hospitals here in the West. Thus the Hindu temples have become religious as well as social centres, and the 1983 leaflet produced by the National Council of Hindu Temples (UK) lists at least 30 temples in cities like Leicester, Preston, Coventry, Leeds, Luton, Rugby, Loughborough, Birmingham, Bristol, Huddersfield, Bradford, Southampton, Ashton-Under-Lyne, Derby, Wolverhampton and Walsall, in addition to the temples in the Greater London districts like Southall, Leytonstone, Hendon, Willesden and Golders Green. In fact, there are over 100 temples in Britain as a whole.

Some of these temples organise language, music and dance classes for Hindu children born here, which go a long way towards creating an awareness and a religious identity among the youngsters. Temples give Hindus an opportunity to worship together as a group and act as a focal point for meeting other Hindus in the locality to discuss social issues affecting their lives in their new land.

One temple fosters the worship of Krishna and the teachings of the *Bhagavadgitā*. Many non-Hindus attend *Janma-Ashtami* celebrations there. The *Vedānta* centre, just outside London, provides discussions, lectures and information about *Vedānta* philosophy. Hindu centres promote the work of *Ārya Samāj*, and the *Vishwa Hindu Parishad* looks after the interests of Hindus on an international basis.

Inevitably the influence of the linguistic or regional majority in each area is seen in British temples and the worship pattern reflects regional traditions back in India. The celebrations of certain festivals also show a regional emphasis; for instance, Marāthi speakers celebrate *Ganesh-chaturthi* with the same fervour as Gujarati speakers celebrate the *Navarātri*, or Hindi speakers celebrate the *Rāma* festival.

A couple of weeks ago we visited a temple in London which is run by a sub-sect in the *Vaishnava* tradition. The *Swaminārāyan* temple and movement are supported by the Gujarati business community and the organisation is quite prosperous. Although clearly a part of Hinduism since they accept the authority of the

Vedas and preach the qualified monism of *Rāmānuja's Vedānta*, the Sect is somewhat unusual because the adherents hope to achieve *Moksha* through worshipping the founder, Sahajānanda (1781–1830), who is believed to have been an incarnation of Lord Vishnu; hence he is known as *Swami Nārāyan*. The present leader is the sixth in a series of successive heads of the movement, which was founded by Sahajānanda in 1824 in Gujarat; the estimated number of followers in Britain is 35 000–40 000. Women have their own separate organisation within the movement.

There are many followers of *Sai Bābā* of Shirdi as well as of *Satya Sai Bābā* living and worshipping in Britain. The estimated number of Hindus in Britain is no more than three *lākhs* (300 000), yet almost all varieties of Hinduism, except perhaps village Hinduism, are practised here with full freedom of worship.

Ganesh and I, with our daughter Sheila, are planning to visit Wāi at the time of the *Ganapati* festival next year to renew not only our family ties but our bond with our *Sanātana Dharma*.

My namaskārs to Ājī, Govind, Yamū, Gopāl and Rādhā, and blessings to Vasant, Gitā, Ramesh, Tārā and Leenā. I am writing a letter to Latā and Mādhav asking them to come to Wāi with their son Mohan when we shall be there, so that the whole family can be together for the festival.

Your affectionate daughter,
Neelā

Ābā laid down his daughter's letter with a sigh of satisfaction; he leaned back, closed his eyes, and, feeling completely at peace, dreamed of his whole family around him again during the year that was to come.

Comparative Time Chart

INDIA		EUROPE
	BC	
Indus Valley civilisation	Before 2000	Aegean civilisation of Crete spreading to Greek States
	1800	Use of bronze and copper. Linear script invented.
Aryan invasions from North-West. Aryans settle and inter-marry with original inhabitants. Early hymns of *Rig Veda*	1600–1400	
	1400	Fall of Crete. Indo-Europeans invade Greece from North.
	12th century	Siege of Troy.
	11th century	Dorians invade Greece.
Growth of Hindu religion. Ideas of *Brahman*, *Moksha* and *Samsāra* formulated. Vedic literature produced. Varna system develops.	10th–9th century	Growth of Greek City States. Cultural unity—Sparta, Corinth, Athens, Thebes. *Iliad* and *Odyssey* composed.

Upanishads composed.	8th century BC	First Olympiad. Founding of Rome.
First philosopher Yājnavalkya (630–583) mentioned in the *Brihadāranyaka Upanishad*	7th century	Invasions of Italy. Etruscans in Rome.
Gautama (563–483) founds *Buddhism*. Mahavira (599–527), founder of the *Jain* sect. Kapila (550–500), founder of *Sāmkhya* philosophy. Gautama (580–520), author of *Nyāya-Sutra*. Sushruta uses magnets in surgery.	6th century	Start of modern philosophy, science and literature. Growth of Athens as a democracy. Pythagoras' Laws of Mathematics. Pole-lathe invented. Magnetic compass used.
Bādarāyana's *Vedānta Sūtras* (440–380). Jaimini (430–370), founder of the *Pūrva Mīmāmsā* school of philosophy.	5th century	Golden Age of Greece. Tragedies of Aeschylus and Sophocles. Age of Pericles. Parthenon built. Socrates born about 469 BC. Plato (427–347). Republic established in Rome.
327 BC Alexander invades North Western India. Pānini composes	4th century	Plato dies in 347. Aristotle born in 384 and dies in 322. Alexander the Great

	BC	
Sanskrit Grammar. 326 BC Chandragupta founds the Mauryan kingdom. *Arthashāstra* written by Kautilya. 302 BC Bindusara, the second Mauryan king succeeds his father, Chandragupta. The Empire grows in strength. *Varna-Āshrama-Dharma* firmly established		(355–323) establishes his Empire. His father Philip dies in 336. Hellenistic Empire in Near and Middle East. Rome becomes supreme in Italy.
Mauryan Empire at its zenith under Ashoka (273–232), who establishes Buddhism over most of India, endows education, builds roads and hospitals. Reign of peace and reform. Most of India united for first time. Patanjali (240–180) writes *Yoga-Sūtras* and possibly *Mahābhāshya* (Great Commentary) on Panini.	3rd century	Two Punic Wars. Rome defeats Carthage (265–211). Euclid writes geometry. Archimedes experiments in physics.
Patanjali dies 180 BC. The Epics, *Rāmāyana* and	2nd century	Third Punic War (153–146). Wars against Macedonia

Mahābhārata, begin to grow in size and influence. Early version in use.	BC	(200–168). Rome conquers Greece.
First few of the 29 caves at Ajantā are excavated in the rock, 250 miles North-East of Bombay. Vikrama Era started from 58 BC. The *Bhagavadgitā* is in use. The Shakas rule a large part of North-West India.	1st century	Roman Republic under Pompey, Caesar and Crassus. Caesar dictator of Rome (48–44). Caesar conquers Gaul and invades Britain. Golden age of literature: Cicero, Virgil, Livy. Caesar killed 44 BC. Octavian defeats Mark Antony. Mark Antony and Queen Cleopatra commit suicide. Octavian becomes the first Roman Emperor as Augustus Caesar from 27 BC.
Rāmāyana attains its full version. *Harivamsha* composed. Mauryan Empire split up into small kingdoms under foreign invaders. King Kanishka AD 100. Hinduism as a unifying factor in this period of political chaos. Influence of *Buddhism* gradually	AD 1st and 2nd centuries	Jesus preaches, and the new religion, Christianity, takes root. Travels of St Paul. *New Testament* written. Advanced systems of Roman Law in force from Spain to Persia. Spread of Graeco–Roman culture. Splendid Roman architecture. Despite

	AD	
fades in India. *Shaka* era founded AD 78. Laws of *Manu* in use.		persecution, Christianity grows steadily. Romans invade Britain.
The *Mahābhārata* includes some reference to the post-Mauryan period. Possibly Patanjali wrote his Commentary on Panini's Grammar. First images of Buddha produced in North-West India.	200–300	Roman Empire divided into Western and Eastern parts. Western Empire gradually declines. Hadrian's Wall renovated AD 210.
Gupta Empire, founded by Chandra-Gupta I, grows in power. Golden age of Indian culture. Sanskrit classical poetry produced by Kalidāsa. Āryabhatta, the astronomer, writes about the round shape of the Earth and its rotation about its axis. Chinese pilgrim Fa-Hsien visits India. White Huns attack the Gupta Empire. *Purāṇas*—the legends and	300–500	St Augustine (AD 334–416). Christianity declared the official religion of the Roman Empire, AD 313. After AD 400, Romans withdrew from Britain. The Saxons begin invading Britain.

	AD	
myths—begin to be written between AD 450 and 550.		
Hindu numerals, place value and zero concept invented; these theories travel to Europe through the Arab traders.	500–600	St Patrick in Ireland 452–461. Christianity reaches Scotland in 563 and Northumbria in AD 635.
King Harsha rules at Kanauj. Chālukya Kingdom in the Deccan, Rajputs in North India. The Pallavas flourish in South India.	600–700	London a centre of commerce. Learning revived by Bede (AD 673–735).
Arabs conquer Sind. Pāla kings rule over Bihar and Bengal in the East. The outstanding scholar Shankara (788–820) writes commentaries on the *Vedānta*	700–800	No clear distinction between Church and State. Offa II rules Mercia (757–796).
and the *Bhagavadgitā*. The Chola kingdom dominates South India.	800–1000	The Vikings begin their raids on Britain. Alfred becomes King of Wessex.
Mahmud of Ghazni raids North India and desecrates Somanāth Temple in Gujarat. Rāmānuja (1040–1137) writes his qualified	1000–1200	Canute, King of England, 1016–1036. Norman conquest of Britain: Battle of Hastings 1066. William King of England

non-dualism version of the *Vedānta*. The Hoysalas rule in South-West India.	AD	1066–1087. William II 1087–1100. Henry I 1100–1135. Church and State conflict under Henry II—Becket murdered.
Muhammad Ghurid establishes a kingdom in North India. Vijayanagar (1336–1565), a Hindu kingdom, flourishes in the South. Mādhava (1199–1260) writes the *dwaita-vedānta* doctrine.	1200–1400	Magna Carta AD 1215. Mechanical clock produced. Firearms produced in China and Europe. Gunpowder in use; it was first invented in China in the tenth century. St Francis of Assisi. St Thomas Aquinas.
Kabir preaches one God for Muslims and Hindus. Baba Nanak (1469–1538) preaches unity of God and rejects formalism of Islam and Hinduism. Vasco da Gama at Calicut.	1400–1500	Printing, first invented in China 1000 BC, used in Europe. Martin Luther (1483–1546).
Goa established as a Portuguese colony. St Francis Xavier in Goa. Babur founds the Mughal Empire in 1526. Akbar consolidates the Empire 1556–1605. Architecture flourishes at Agra Fort and Sikri.	1500–1600	Henry VIII breaks away from Rome. The Church of England, a Protestant form of Christianity, established. The Reformation. Queen Elizabeth I rules England. The Spanish Armada

	AD	
		fails to invade Britain.
European powers compete for trade concessions. Hindu political and religious resurgence in Western India under Shivāji. Shah Jahan builds the Taj Mahal. Shivāji revives Hindu coronation ceremony (1674) after a lapse of 1000 years. Hindus—Marāthās— fight the Mughals in defence of their country and religion.	1600–1700	Calculating machine invented by Pascal, 1642. Magic lantern invented 1668. Pressure cooker invented 1680. Steam engine invented by Watt. Telescope developed in Italy, 1609. British East India Company established.
Mughal power in decline after 1707. Marāthā expansion into North and Central India. The British, under Clive, win at Plassey in 1757 and extend their power to gain political supremacy.	1700–1800	Sewing machine first manufactured. Submarines built. Thermometer to measure degrees of heat invented. Clive wins at Plassey and lays the foundation of British power in India.
The Marāthās defeated by the British. The Sikhs rule over the Punjab as independent king-	1800–1900	Science and technology: Anaesthetics—Morton 1846 (USA). Bicycle —1879. Cameras

dom until 1848. *Brahmo Samāj* founded. The great rebellion—Indian Mutiny—in 1857. The British possessions in India come under the government of the Crown. First fingerprint in Bengal by Sir William Herschel. Indian National Congress, founded in 1885, begins its activities for Independence. Rāmakrishna Paramahamsa (1836–1886). Rabindranāth Tagore (1861–1941). Vivekānanda (1863–1902) presents Hinduism as a world religion. Dayānanda founds the *Arya Samāj*. Gandhi (1869–1948) trains as a lawyer and goes to South Africa. Shri Aurobindo (1872–1950). Dr Rādhākrishnan (1888–1975). Syed Ahmad Khan puts forward the two-nation theory in 1888.

AD 1800–1900

and first photograph 1826. Dynamo—Faraday 1831. Gramophone—Edison 1878. Paper-making machine—1803. Plastics—1833. Pneumatic tyre—Dunlop 1888. Railways. Reaping machines. Refrigerator—1834 Rubber. Stethoscope. Telegraph—1845. Telephone—1876. Typewriter—1876. Napoleon Emperor of France in 1804. Napoleon defeated at Waterloo in 1815. British Empire at its zenith at the turn of the century. Hinduism confidently declares itself as a world faith.

	AD 1900–1987	
The Muslim League is formed in 1906. Congress is still a middle-class movement, until Gandhi, on his return from South Africa in 1915, turns it into a people's movement for Indian Independence. Jallianwala Bagh massacre in 1919. Gandhi launches *Satyāgraha*—passive resistence—movements against the British, based on Truth (*Satya*) and (*Ahimsā*) non-injury. Gandhi's great march against Salt Tax. Round Table Conference in London. Dr Iqbal proposes creation of Pakistan in 1930. Congress starts 'Quit India' movement in 1942. Calcutta killings in 1946. India and Pakistan: new states. Indian Independence 1947. Nehru first Prime Minister.		Aeroplane—Wright brothers 1903. Russian Revolution—1917. Finger-printing used at Scotland Yard—1901. Motor car: mass production—1910. Nylon—1928. Radio: speech and music—1906. Television–Baird 1926. Thermos flask invented. Electric torch—1914. Tractor—1902. Vacuum cleaner—1903. The Great War 1914–18. The Second World War 1939–45. Atomic fission. Atomic bomb. Britain withdraws from India in 1947. Jet aeroplanes for civil aviation. Queen Elizabeth II reigns in Britain after 1952. International radio telephones. Space flight. First man on the moon.

States reorganised on linguistic basis between 1956 and 1960.
Nehru dies 1964.
Indira Gandhi assassinated 1984.
Bangladesh created in 1971.
India a secular state since Independence.

AD

Glossary

Advaita Vedānta: Non-dualistic philosophy of Shankara which holds that the supreme spirit, *Brahman*, and the individual soul, *Ātman*, are identical.

Ahimsā: 'Non-injury'—based on compassion for all creatures.

Arjuna: Pandu warrior prince who was advised on 'Disinterested Action' by Krishna in the *Bhagavadgitā*.

Artha: One of the four basic aims in life. They are *Dharma* (duty), *Artha* (acquiring the means of life), *Kāma* (enjoyment of the sense objects) and *Moksha* (final release from the cycle of birth and death).

Āryans: Nomadic pastoralists who invaded India before 1500 BC, bringing with them the early Vedic culture.

Ārya Samāj: Society founded by Dayānanda (1824–1883) to revive Vedic culture in India.

Āsana: Yoga posture used to control the body and the mind.

Ashrama: Stage in life. The four *āshramas* are *Brahmacharya*, *Grihastha*, *Vānaprastha* and *Sannyās*.

Atharva Veda: One of the Vedas, the revealed scriptures of the Hindus.

Ātman: The individual Self, or Soul.

AUM: Sacred syllable containing the sound of all reality —*Brahman*.

Aurobindo: Hindu mystic famous for his writings on yoga.

Avatār: An incarnation of God, particularly of Lord Vishnu.

Bhagavadgitā: Literally 'the Song of the Lord', a popular sacred text of Hinduism.

Bhakti Mārga: Literally 'path of devotion', a way to achieve *Moksha* through devotional self-surrender to a personal god, Īshvara.

Brahmā: God, as the creative energy of the Supreme Spirit.

Brahmacharya: The first stage of life, devoted to celibacy and the study of the *Vedas*.

Brahman: Ultimate Reality, the Supreme Spirit.

Brāhmana: The portion of the *Vedas* describing sacrifice and other rituals.

Brahma Sūtras: The basic teachings of the *Upanishads*, the foundation of the Vedānta.

Brahmin: A member of the first *Varna*, consisting of priests and professionals.

Brahmo Samāj: Society founded in 1828 by Rām Mohan Roy to reform Hinduism.

Deva: The Sanskrit word for God.

Devatā: A minor deity, such as those worshipped in Indian villages.

Devi: A goddess, such as Pārvati or Laxmi.

Dharma: Moral duty in accordance with one's *Varna*, *Āshrama*, *Kula* and *Jāti*. The first aim in life.

Dhoti: A piece of cotton or silk cloth, six yards long and five feet wide, worn by men around the lower part of the body.

Dhyāna: Meditation in Yoga or Bhaktī.

Gandhi: Mohandās K Gandhi, the leader of the Indian Independence Movement, noted for his *satyāgraha*, *ie* insistence upon the truth in practical affairs.

Ganesha: The elephant-headed God, remover of obstacles. Also known as *Ganapati*.

Grihastha: A householder. The second stage in life.

Gunas: the three qualities—*Sattva*, *Rajas* and *Tamas*—of all material and mental existence.

Guru: A personal spiritual guide.

Indra: A principal Indo-Aryan deity of the *Vedas*.

Indra's dart: A special arrow given by Indra to Rāma for the destruction of Rāvana.

Indus: A major river in the North-Western part of the Subcontinent; *Sindhu* is the Sanskrit equivalent.

Īshvara: Brahman personified.

Jāti: One's caste, or place in society, determined by occupation and birth.

Jnāna Mārga: The path of the Knowledge of Brahman, leading to liberation.

Kālī: Goddess Pārvati in her terrifying form.

Kāma: Enjoyment in all its forms. The third aim in life.

Karma Mārga: The path of Action, a means of liberation as long as the fruits of action are not desired.

Krishna: An incarnation of Vishnu embodying joy, freedom and love.

Kshatriya: A member of the second (warrior) *Varna*.

Laxmi: Goddess of Wealth and Good Fortune, consort of Vishnu.

Mahābhārata: The great epic of India containing 100 000 verses in 18 chapters called *parva*.

Mantra: A sacred formula, always Sanskrit.

Manu: The writer of a code of conduct called *Manu Smriti*.

Mīmāmsā: A school of Hindu philosophy founded by Jaimini.

Pandit: A learned Hindu priest.

Pārvati: The Mother Goddess, consort of Shiva. Also called *Ambā*, *Bhavāni*, *Durgā* and *Kālī*.

Prakriti: The Non-Spiritual Reality—Matter.

Prasād: 'Blessed offering' distributed at the end of a Hindu *pūjā*.

Pūjā: Offerings of kum-kum (red powder), rice grains, fruit, flowers, water, incense and light made to an image of a personal deity.

Purusha: The Cosmic Person, or 'First Man', from whom the *varnas* originated.

Purushārtha: Basic aim in life (see *Artha*).

Rādhā: Krishna's divine lover.

Rāma: An incarnation of Vishnu, the hero of the *Rāmāyana*.

Rāmānuja: Eleventh century philosopher famed for his *Vishishta-Advaita* interpretation of the *Upanishads*.

Rāmāyana: The epic poem narrating the story of *Rāma*.

Rig Veda: A collection of about 10 000 hymns representing the oldest Indo-European literature and the foundation of much Indian thought.

Samādhi: Union of the Self with the Ultimate Reality.

Sāmaveda: Hymns for singing in ritual performance.

Sāmkhya: A school of Hindu philosophy.

Samsāra: Cycle of repeating deaths and births.

Samskāra: A purifying rite of passage performed at important junctures in the life of a Hindu.

Sannyāsin: A person who has abandoned all worldly concerns to devote his life to spirituality in the fourth stage in life.

Saraswatī: Goddess of Learning and the Arts, consort of Brahmā, the Creator.

Satya: Truth.

Satyāgraha: Insistence upon the truth in practical affairs.

Shaivism: A cult in which Shiva is worshipped as the principal God.

Shakti: Energy. Personified as a goddess and usually associated with the God Shiva, as the divine energy of his being.

Shiva: The destructive and regenerative manifestation of *Brahman* in the Hindu *Trimūrty—Brahmā*, *Vishnu* and *Shiva*.

Shruti: That which is revealed. The *Vedas*. The infallible truth.

Shūdra: The artisans, forming the fourth *Varna*.

Sita: Consort of Rāma. Ideal of Hindu female marital fidelity.

Smriti: The tradition which is remembered. The books on *dharmashāstras* are included in the *Smritis*.

Sūtra: Aphorism expressing the essence of a teaching: *eg Brahma Sūtra, Grihya Sūtra, Shrauta Sūtra, Vedānta Sūtra*.

Trimūrty: The collective iconographic representation of the three major deities of Hinduism—Brahmā, Vishnu and Shiva.

Upanishads: A collection of secret tutorials about the nature of Ātman, Brahman and the Universe. The concluding portion of the Vedic literature, hence known as the *Vedānta*.

Vaisheshika: The pluralistic school of philosophy.

Vaishnava: A devotee of Vishnu. A member of the *Vaishnava* sect.

Vaishya: The third *Varna*, engaged in commerce and agriculture.

Vānaprastha: The third, or retirement, stage in life.

Varna: A social class based on personal attributes and functions. The *Varna* classification has Vedic authority.

Vedānta: Writings at the end of the *Vedas*. The *Upanishads*. Also a system of philosophy based on the *Upanishads*.

Vedas: The sacred writings of the Indo-Aryans. The scriptural basis of Hinduism.

Vishnu: The second in the *Trimūrty* of Brahmā, Vishnu and Shiva. Vishnu is the preserver of the Universe. He has manifested himself in nine *Avatārs*. The last one—*Kalki*—is still to come.

Yajna: Sacrifice in which offerings are made to Agni, the presiding deity of the sacred fire.

Yajur Veda: The text for the ritual performance of *yajna*.

Yama: The Spirit of Death.

Yoga: A system of philosophy and exercises. A discipline for overcoming bondage and suffering.

Further Reading

Patricia Bahree, *Hinduism* (Batsford, London, 1984)
Patricia Bahree, *The Hindu World* (Macdonald Educational, London, 1982)
A L Basham, *The Wonder that was India* (Sidgwick and Jackson, London, 1985)
P Bowes, *The Hindu Religious Tradition* (Routledge & Kegan Paul Ltd, London, 1978)
M Chatterjēe, *Gandhi's Religious Thought* (Macmillan, London, 1985)
Swami Harshananda, *Hindu Gods and Goddesses* (Ramakrishna Ashram Mysore, 1981) (Available from Ramakrishna Vedanta Centre, Bourne End, Buckinghamshire SL8 5LG)
H A Kanitkar, *Hindus in Britain* (School of Oriental and African Studies, London, 1982)
V P (Hemant) Kanitkar, *Hindu Festivals and Sacraments* (Barnet, 1984) (Available from Arthur Probsthain, Oriental Booksellers, 41 Great Russell Street, London WC1B 3PH)
V P (Hemant) Kanitkar, *Hinduism* (Wayland, Hove, 1985)
V P (Hemant) Kanitkar, *Hindu Stories* (Wayland, Hove, 1986)
V P (Hemant) Kanitkar, *Indian Food and Drink* (Wayland, Hove, 1986)
Kim Knott, *Hinduism in Leeds* (University of Leeds, 1986)
Juan Mascaro, *The Bhagavadgitā* (Penguin, Harmondsworth, 1962)
J Nehru, *The Discovery of India* (Meridian Books, London, 1956)
Wendy D O'Flaherty, *Hindu Myths* (Penguin, Harmondsworth, 1981)
S Radhakrishnan and C A Moore, *Sourcebook of Indian Philosophy* (Princeton University Press, Princeton, USA, 1973)
A Ramachandran, *Hanumān* (A & C Black, London, 1979)

Swami Sivananda, *Bhagavadgītā: Text and Commentary* (Sivanand Press, Durban, South Africa, 1968) (Available from Human Service Trust, Krishnashram, 10 Wilson Gardens, Harrow HA1 4DZ)